POWER SALES WORDS

How to Write It, Say It, and
Sell It with Sizzle

Vicky Oliver

SOURCEBOOKS, INC.
NAPERVILLE, ILLINOIS

Published by Sourcebooks, Inc.
P.O. Box 4410, Naperville, Illinois 60567-4410
(630) 961-3900
Fax: (630) 961-2168
www.sourcebooks.com

Library of Congress Cataloging-in-Publication Data
Oliver, Vicky
Power sales words : how to write it, say it, and sell it with sizzle / Vicky Oliver.
p. cm.
ISBN-13: 978-1-4022-0650-4
ISBN-10: 1-4022-0650-X
1. Advertising copy. 2. Marketing. I. Title.
HF5825.O45 2006
659.13'2—dc22

2005033341
Printed and bound in the United States of America
CH 10 9 8 7 6 5 4 3 2 1

This book is dedicated to my grandmother Janice, who always had an irrepressible curiosity about my writing. Many times, she would "cordially demand" that I send her hard copies of the ads I had written (and being a dutiful granddaughter, I had no choice but to comply). Her passion inspired me, and I hope that in some small way, it will also touch all those who read this book.

chiseled crotchety ecstatic conscientious genuine dour gripping magnetic nagging erratic spiri
ky tenacity congenial titillating risque haughty enduring svelte poignant eccentric rich achieve as
lenge chop clarify commit craft create dramatize enhance erase finagle find finesse generate ins
rrogate interrupt jump lead motivate nip organize oversee pepper pinch plan raise rally rouse s
e strategize surpass trump tweeze unveil win zoom striking appalling deadly manic inspired bleak r
d disastrous exhilarating captivating outstanding wry chiseled crotchety ecstatic conscientious g
dour gripping magnetic nagging erratic spiritual cocky tenacity congenial titillating risque haug
uring svelte poignant eccentric rich achieve aspire challenge chop clarify commit craft create dra
enhance erase finagle find finesse generate inspire interrogate interrupt jump lead motivate nip org
oversee pepper pinch plan raise rally rouse save shake strategize surpass trump tweeze unveil
n striking appalling deadly manic inspired bleak rigid jaded disastrous exhilarating captivating
ding wry chiseled crotchety ecstatic conscientious genuine dour gripping magnetic nagging err
tual cocky tenacity congenial titillating risque haughty enduring svelte poignant eccentric rich achi
re challenge chop clarify commit craft create dramatize enhance erase finagle find finesse gene
ire interrogate interrupt jump lead motivate nip organize oversee pepper pinch plan raise rally ro
shake strategize surpass trump tweeze unveil win zoom striking appalling deadly manic inspired bl
jaded disastrous exhilarating captivating outstanding wry chiseled crotchety ecstatic conscienti
uine dour gripping magnetic nagging erratic spiritual cocky tenacity congenial titillating risque haug
uring svelte poignant eccentric rich achieve aspire challenge chop clarify commit craft create dra
enhance erase finagle find finesse generate inspire interrogate interrupt jump lead motivate nip org
oversee pepper pinch plan raise rally rouse save shake strategize surpass trump tweeze unveil
n striking appalling deadly manic inspired bleak rigid jaded disastrous exhilarating captivating
ding wry chiseled crotchety ecstatic conscientious genuine dour gripping magnetic nagging err
tual cocky tenacity congenial titillating risque haughty enduring svelte poignant eccentric rich achi
re challenge chop clarify commit craft create dramatize enhance erase finagle find finesse gene
ire interrogate interrupt jump lead motivate nip organize oversee pepper pinch plan raise rally ro
shake nip striking appalling deadly manic inspired bleak rigid jaded disastrous exhilarating capti
outstanding wry chiseled crotchety ecstatic conscientious genuine dour gripping magnetic nagg
tic spiritual cocky tenacity congenial titillating risque haughty enduring svelte poignant eccentric
eve aspire challenge chop clarify commit craft create dramatize enhance erase finagle find fine
erate inspire interrogate interrupt jump lead motivate nip organize oversee pepper pinch plan raise r
e save shake strategize surpass trump tweeze unveil win zoom striking appalling deadly manic insp
k rigid jaded disastrous exhilarating captivating outstanding wry chiseled crotchety ecstatic consc

Contents

*Acknowledgments

My heartfelt thanks to Bethany Brown for leaping over obstacles like a modern day super-heroine to get this book made; to June Clark for her "never call it quits" energy, zeal, and drive; and to every boss I've ever had in advertising—particularly those mentors from my cub copy-writer days who nitpicked with me endlessly about pesky details like commas and exclamation points. Somewhere along the way, I learned how to write advertising copy. Thank you, one and all.

...nsoled crotchety ecstatic conscientious genuine dour gripping magnetic nagging erratic spi...
...y tenacity congenial titillating risque haughty enduring svelte poignant eccentric rich achieve as
...lenge chop clarify commit craft create dramatize enhance erase finagle find finesse generate ins
...rogate interrupt jump lead motivate nip organize oversee pepper pinch plan raise rally rouse s
...e strategize surpass trump tweeze unveil win zoom striking appalling deadly manic inspired bleak r
...d disastrous exhilarating captivating outstanding wry chiseled crotchety ecstatic conscientious g
...dour gripping magnetic nagging erratic spiritual cocky tenacity congenial titillating risque hau
...uring svelte poignant eccentric rich achieve aspire challenge chop clarify commit craft create dra
...enhance erase finagle find finesse generate inspire interrogate interrupt jump lead motivate nip org
...oversee pepper pinch plan raise rally rouse save shake strategize surpass trump tweeze unveil
...n striking appalling deadly manic inspired bleak rigid jaded disastrous exhilarating captivating
...ding wry chiseled crotchety ecstatic conscientious genuine dour gripping magnetic nagging err
...tual cocky tenacity congenial titillating risque haughty enduring svelte poignant eccentric rich ach
...re challenge chop clarify commit craft create dramatize enhance erase finagle find finesse gene
...ire interrogate interrupt jump lead motivate nip organize oversee pepper pinch plan raise rally ro
...shake strategize surpass trump tweeze unveil win zoom striking appalling deadly manic inspired b
...jaded disastrous exhilarating captivating outstanding wry chiseled crotchety ecstatic conscient
...uine dour gripping magnetic nagging erratic spiritual cocky tenacity congenial titillating risque hau
...uring svelte poignant eccentric rich achieve aspire challenge chop clarify commit craft create dra
...enhance erase finagle find finesse generate inspire interrogate interrupt jump lead motivate nip org
...oversee pepper pinch plan raise rally rouse save shake strategize surpass trump tweeze unveil
...n striking appalling deadly manic inspired bleak rigid jaded disastrous exhilarating captivating
...ding wry chiseled crotchety ecstatic conscientious genuine dour gripping magnetic nagging err
...tual cocky tenacity congenial titillating risque haughty enduring svelte poignant eccentric rich ach
...re challenge chop clarify commit craft create dramatize enhance erase finagle find finesse gene
...ire interrogate interrupt jump lead motivate nip organize oversee pepper pinch plan raise rally ro
...e shake nip striking appalling deadly manic inspired bleak rigid jaded disastrous exhilarating capti
...outstanding wry chiseled crotchety ecstatic conscientious genuine dour gripping magnetic nag...
...tic spiritual cocky tenacity congenial titillating risque haughty enduring svelte poignant eccentric
...eve aspire challenge chop clarify commit craft create dramatize enhance erase finagle find fine
...erate inspire interrogate interrupt jump lead motivate nip organize oversee pepper pinch plan raise
...e save shake strategize surpass trump tweeze unveil win zoom striking appalling deadly manic insp
...k rigid jaded disastrous exhilarating captivating outstanding wry chiseled crotchety ecstatic consc
...s genuine dour gripping magnetic nagging erratic spiritual cocky tenacity congenial titillating ris

The 12 Laws of Writing Compelling Copy

1. **Decide your message**. Take a piece of paper and write down your goal in compelling language. It can be one sentence: "My goal is to convince the XYZ company to buy seventeen thousand widgets from my company," or "My goal is to persuade MSNBC to put me on their morning show," or "My goal is to land a job at Big, Gargantuan, & Humongous Advertising, even though I've never written a piece of advertising copy before."

2. **Devise a strategy**. In one simple sentence, write down what your strategy is. In plain English, this is why anyone should care. Use motivating, empowering language and phrase your strategy to make it sound as if your dream has already happened. "MSNBC is so excited about the seminars that I have been teaching that I get a slot on their morning show." In this example, your letter to MSNBC will need to describe what's appealing about your seminars in clear, crisp language. Why should hundreds of people stop doing whatever is pressing today, pick up the phone, and enroll in your seminars immediately? Commit your strategy to the same piece of paper as your message. Then tack the paper up on your wall with some removable scotch tape. (Don't worry. The paint won't chip. That's why you're using *removable* scotch tape.)

3. **Keep it simple**. Pare down your message until it is crystal clear. Remember that your primary job is always to persuade someone to take action, and don't let too many words get in the

way. Never fixate on what the correct length of a piece of copy should be. Great copy is like a skirt. It should be long enough to cover the subject and short enough to be interesting. The first section of this book will give you all of the tools that you need to simplify your copy. It's now time to take out a second piece of paper and begin writing your first draft.

4. **Don't be afraid to be provocative.** Open with a question, an interesting idea, an irresistible challenge, or a novel thought. "If money can't buy happiness, why does everyone always wish they had more of it?" The second section of this book will help you write copy that commands people's attention and forces them to take notice.

5. **Know your audience.** Even if you are writing an article for a magazine with a circulation of one hundred thousand, you are always talking to one reader at a time. Picture that person in your mind's eye. Is she well educated? Does she have a sense of humor, or is she more seriously inclined? Match your copy style to your reader's style. If your reader went to Harvard Business School, you can use longer words and more complicated syntax than if you are writing to a woman who never attended college.

6. **Find your voice—and stick to it.** For business writing, it's often helpful to write copy almost as if you were speaking the same set of words. This will keep your copy brisk. As a general rule, the language of persuasion should not be flowery or sound like it came out of the *Bureaucrat's Thesaurus.*

7. **Eliminate the bells and whistles.** Why? Aren't bells and whistles what great copy is all about? Maybe in an alternate universe where everyone is a hack. But on this planet, bells, whistles, and cutesy punctuation only get in the way. Once you've nixed the bells and whistles, you're ready to commit your longhand document to your computer. Wow! You've been

at this writing thing for perhaps half an hour, and already you have a first draft! Congratulations. But don't stop there.

8. **Choose your words wisely**. There are over 175,000 words in the English language. Many of them mean almost the same thing. On the one hand, that gives you a lot of variety—the spice of great writing. On the other hand, even a brilliant message has the potential to get lost in clichés. The fifth section of this book will help you fine-tune your word selection so that you can say what you mean and mean what you say. This is the essence of good, strong, clear communication. Do not ignore this vital step.

9. **Edit, edit, edit**. Then, go back and revise and tweak. When you are 100 percent certain that your copy is absolutely brilliant, put it through the grinder one last time and polish it. Then, show it to a really great writer and have him look at it with a critical eye. Sometimes, editing your copy will involve eliminating repetition and redundancy. (Whoops! Those two words mean the same thing.) Or perhaps you will need to take your cleverest line and eliminate it. (Ouch! That one particularly hurts.)

10. **Sleep on it**. This may be challenging if you used a tight deadline to get over your fear of the blank page. You're out of time…you don't have the time to give it twenty-four more hours, right? Wrong. Even in the 24/7 world that we inhabit, you can always wrangle one extra day if you really need it. "My computer is down," or "My local FedEx office is closed today for some reason. Can I *please* have one more day to get you that sales pitch?" will usually suffice to give you the time you need.

11. **Review your copy one last time**. Make sure that your main message is coming through loud and clear. Review your strategy statement as well. Did you conform to it? Spell check

your document twice—once for typos and grammar and a second time for usage and commonly confused words. You'll find a list of them in the appendix of this book.

12. **Let your copy fly**. You've done it. When it comes to writing copy, you are a master. It's time to let others enjoy your words. Release your copy to the universe, and watch it work wonders for you.

How to Use This Book

There are two ways to use this book. You can use it as a step-by-step, "how to" kit on the craft of copywriting. Or you can use it as a brain tease to kick-start the creative process and get those words flowing.

If you have never written a piece of copy before, you will benefit enormously by reading this book once through, section by section. Doing so will give you the lay of the land in terms of what any piece of copy needs to cover. You'll learn how to keep your message simple but compelling and how to choose the words that will clarify your key idea.

If, on the other hand, you are a seasoned writer, feel free to skip around this book whenever there's a specific writing problem that nags you. Is your lead long and rambling? Are you having trouble finding the perfect verb? Are you experiencing a "punctuation moment," saddling your words with exclamation points and quotes, double dashes and semicolons? Is your copy screaming with adjectives, making you sound like a used car salesman instead of a respectable self-promoter? This book will help you become unstuck.

Keep it as a handy reference, near your computer, bedside, shower, or anyplace where you come up with ideas. You'll find that this book will unblock writer's block, so you might want to also lend it occasionally to other deserving members of the tribe.

The Fear Factor

(Or Copywriting 101 for Anyone Who Has to Write Almost Anything)

It's the moment of truth. You have an assignment to write a persuasive piece of copy. But instead of writing down even one word, you are just sitting there, staring at a blank piece of paper. Maybe you've been looking at it for just ten minutes. Possibly, you've been gazing at it for over an hour. You feel lost and dazed. But the good news is that you are not alone.

You're simply experiencing the same daunting obstacle that all writers confront at some point in their careers: fear of the blank page.

Whether you happen to be a professional copywriter with years of experience under your belt, a marketer with a specific product to sell, a salesperson with a pitch due tomorrow morning, or a job hunter who is struggling to capture your strengths on a one-page resume, you will have to face down this personal demon.

The trick is to simply get started. And right here you have all of the tools that you need to begin. Are you groping for a gripping lead? Turn to section II, and learn how to make your copy provocative. Do you need a riveting way to position your product or service? Skim section IV, "Closing Arguments." It will help you construct your message on a solid foundation of truth. Are you convinced that one pithy phrase would capture absolutely everything you needed to say if you could only find the elusive words? Review section V, "Choose Your Words Wisely." Words are the bait and tackle of writing persuasive copy, and there are thousands in this volume for you to experiment with.

Think of this book as your vocabulary toolbox, and you can use it to build a compelling, puncture-proof case for any product or service. Or you can use it to chop your way through writer's block—one dead piece of language at a time. There are motivating verbs to structure your sentences. There are scissors to help you trim your copy. You'll even find simple "how to" instructions every step of the way.

Take courage from the fact that writing copy is a craft and not an innate talent. Because it is a craft, it can be learned, and then polished. So while you're still feeling brave, let's get started. Fear or no fear, you are about to write the most persuasive piece of copy that you've ever crafted!

Section I:
Keep It Simple

Wordiness is ponderous, not to mention pompous and bombastic. Whether you are writing a business plan, a job-hunting letter, some elegant copy for one of your clients, or some prose, excess verbiage only gets in the way. Think of your copy as an onion, and keep peeling off layers until you arrive at the essential message. Or, if onions make you cry, think of your message as a diamond in the rough. You're a writer, so feel free to pick your own metaphor to describe your copy. But keep simplifying your message until it is clear, concise, and motivating.

There are five ways to keep your message simple.

1. Put Your Copy on a Strict Adjective Diet
2. Be Active, Not Passive
3. Dispense with the Fluff and the Frou-Frou
4. Stop Dancing around What You Are Trying to Say
5. Don't Fall into the Redundancy Trap

No worries. You can put your copy on a strict adjective diet and still stuff your face with pasta.

1. Put Your Copy on a Strict Adjective Diet

Resist the temptation to fill up on empty adjectives. One good adjective is worth ten puffed up ones—providing your copy with the daily minimum requirement without any hideous trans fat. Use all adjectives sparingly and make every single one of them count. If you need extra help with word selection, check out the Synonym Finder at the back of this book. But remember, as with all diets, a strict adjective diet depends on portion control, so no cheating! Addicted to adjectives? Adjective Watchers Anonymous meets bi-weekly.

Lame adjectives	Can Be Rephrased...
attractive	striking
average, as in "the average man"	most men
awesome	awe-inspiring
bad	appalling
ballsy	chutzpah*
beautiful	chic
boring	deadly
conservative	right-wing
cool**	fashion-forward
costly	obscenely expensive
crazy	manic
deep (as in "thought-provoking")	inspired
depressing	bleak
difficult	rigid

cynical	jaded
dumb (as in "ill-advised")	disastrous
entertaining	hilarious
evil	wicked
exciting**	exhilarating
fabulous**	captivating
first-rate	outstanding
funny	wry
great body	chiseled
grumpy	crotchety
handsome	Adonis
happy	ecstatic
hardworking	conscientious
honest	genuine
humorless	dour
incredible	gripping
intelligent**	pure genius
interesting	magnetic
irritating	nagging
moody***	erratic
narcissistic	self-involved
new-age	spiritual
over-confident	cocky

persistent	tenacity
pleasant	congenial
sexy	titillating
slutty	risqué
snobby	haughty
solid**	enduring
sweet!	superb
thin	svelte
touching	poignant
tragically hip	fashion victim
unlucky	star-crossed
weird	eccentric
well-to-do	rich

*See "Yiddish That's Made Its Way into Spoken English," Section V, 13.
**Check out the Synonym Finder in the Appendix.
***See "Words That Get You in the Mood (Not *That* Mood)," Section V, 14.

WATCH YOUR LANGUAGE

There are three types of adjectives that you should avoid in your copy: adjectives that are slang (the word "phat" has too many calories per letter), adjectives that are as bland as toast (How "thin" is she? Is she svelte or anorexic?), and adjectives that have lost their meaning through overuse, like the word "awesome." Want to add muscle to your copy? Try changing an adjective like the word "persistent" to a noun like "tenacity." Got that? Awesome!

2. Be Active, Not Passive

Declarative sentences create energy. Passive sentences induce sleepiness faster than a hypnotist. They just lie motionless on the page while your readers drift off into oblivion. Goodbye, readers! Always remember, passive sentences desperately need a ruthless editor—they're too passive to eliminate themselves. Be aggressive about striking the passive voice from your text. (Just try not to be passive-aggressive about it.) Review the action verbs below, then seize your pen and start rewriting.

achieve	exercise
aspire	explain
brainstorm	finagle
challenge	find
chop	fine-tune
clarify	finesse
commit	finish
craft	generate
create	inspire
compete	interrogate
complete	interrupt
customize	introduce
cut	investigate
develop	jump
discover	kick-start
dramatize	lead
eliminate	meet
enhance	motivate
erase	nip

open
organize
oversee
pepper
pinch
plan
prepare
prevail
promise
promote
raise
rally
release
review
rise
rouse
save
seize
shake

shape
sharpen
shine
snoop
spearhead
star
stir
strategize
surpass
tear
trounce
trump
tweeze
uncover
unveil
win
work
zoom

Word Up
This just in from our distinguished panel of English language buffs. Compare and contrast the sentence "She works hard for the money" with "The money was hard to come by." In the first sentence, the subject (she) performs an action. In the second sentence, the subject (the money) is acted upon. The first sentence is declarative; the second sentence is passive. There will be a pop quiz later.

3. Dispense with the Fluff and the Frou-Frou

The list of people counseling writers to keep their prose short is long indeed. The mathematician Blaise Pascal once wrote, "If I had more time, I would write a shorter letter." The philosopher Baltasar Gracian wrote, "Good things, when short, are twice as good." The playwright William Shakespeare summed up the sentiment even more succinctly with "Brevity is the soul of wit." (And these guys were counseling writers to edit their prose centuries ago when there was nothing to do but read!) Want the long story short? To trim your business solicitations, avoid needless hemming and hawing and the following list of unnecessary words:

absolutely
Actually,
Additionally,
"And let me simply conclude by saying…"
And so it seems,
And that's the way the cookie crumbles.
And where does that leave us today?
And while we're on the topic…
And without further ado,
And yet,
As of this date,
assisted in the development of
At some point in the near future,
at the present time
at which time
BTW:

blah, blah, blah

But still, for some reason...

But to return to the topic before it gels,

By the way,

by virtue of the fact that

Come to think of it,

completely

Considering the fact that...

constantly

Contrary to popular belief,

Due to unforeseen changes in the marketplace,

During the time that

Ergo,

Essentially,

et cetera, et cetera

For starters,

Furthermore,

"I am keen to hear your thoughts. But first,"

I applaud your efforts, but...

"I defer to the esteemed senator from South Carolina."

I look forward to addressing that down the road.

If the situation were reversed,

In a word,

In brief,

In lieu of the fact that,

In reference to the subject that we discussed last week,

In spite of the fact that...

In sum,

In the end, this much was clear:

Ipso facto,

It all comes down to this:

"It goes without saying that..."

Let me get straight to the point:

Let's pause for a moment to consider...

Let's put it this way:

_____ makes an interesting case, but...

miscellaneous

Moreover,

No offense, but...

not to mention...

Now before you jump to any conclusions,

On the plus side:

one might say,

pertaining to

plus which,

regarding the topic that

speaking of,

subsequent to

The question as to whether

Then again,

Therefore,

"There's no easy way to say this, so…"

This is a subject that

This much is clear:

Thus,

totally*

Under the circumstances,

"What can you say about a man who needs no introduction?"

yada, yada, yada

*See "Valley Girlisms," Section V, 13.

LANGUAGE POLICE

Let me just say for the record that today, only trial lawyers can get away with using phrases that are this pompous. The rest of us are better off writing what we mean without first clearing our throats (ahem!). Phew! I'm happy that I got that off my chest. But let me just say for the record that…

4. Stop Dancing Around What You Are Trying to Say

In spoken language, sometimes a few extra flounces can make you sound gracious. So the next time you find yourself at a junior cotillion, feel free to dress up your speech with some telltale formalities of a bygone era. Every gal needs to indulge her inner Scarlett O'Hara sometimes. But frankly, my dear, in written language, even one superfluous flounce can make your copy sound like it's teetering on the verge of extinction. The white gloves have to come off, not to mention those cumbersome hoop skirts! Avoid quaint, old-fashioned phrases that waltz around the mulberry bush, such as:

Are you, perchance, free on…?

Are you quite certain that…?

"Hello?"*

How would you feel about…?

I was hoping that…

I was wondering if…

I would be delighted to escort you…

It was one of those moments when…

May I inquire if…?

May I offer you…?

May I request the pleasure of this dance?

Might I be so bold as to suggest…?

Might I encourage…?

Might I propose…?

Might I trouble you for…?

Might you be interested in…?

Perhaps you may be thinking that...
Recalling those early years,
What would you say if...?
Would you be available to...?
Would you be keen to...?
Would you be so kind as to...?
Would you honor me with...?
Would you kindly consider...?
Would you mind terribly if I...?

*See "Valley Girlisms," Section V, 13.

Word Up
Don't put the word "do" in front of phrases, unless you are applying for a job writing the announcement copy on airplanes. In which case, *do* fasten your seat belt and *do* enjoy your stay.

5. Don't Fall into the Redundancy Trap

Redundancy slows down copy until it moves at the pace of a tortoise. Redundancy slows down copy until it moves at the pace of a tortoise. To repeat, redund—well, you get the basic idea! While the tortoise beat the hare in the fable, in real life, the hare always wins by at least a hair, and nobody has the patience for copy that drags. In business writing, strive for a clean, brisk pace. Keep the momentum flowing, and seek new ways to strike repetition from your writing. Avoid those unwieldy phrases that make your copy plod to a full stop, while your competitor's copy makes sales multiply faster than two hares in heat.

A long, long time ago,

absolutely free of charge

all kinds of different people

As I said before, I never repeat myself.

effectuated action

Every so often, he occasionally remembered to phone home.

He began to keep a diary of the events as he saw them.

He came from a poor family in Iowa. But from his humble beginnings,

He had the worst Peter Pan complex. He just refused to grow up!

He was a total rake. A womanizer with a PhD in philandering.

He was contentious, always stirring up trouble wherever he went.

He was especially unique.

Her marriage had become dull and routine. No doubt about it, she and Richard
were in a rut.

In the beginning, I started to...

Instant replay!

It's been doubly reinforced, so it's twice as strong.

"Just give me a tiny, little slice!" she begged.

Let's circle back to that in a moment.

Let's restate that in a more positive way.

Many, many years ago,

Men: if you say that you're going to call, call!

Mirror, mirror, on the wall,

Not to beat a dead horse, but...

Now let's take a new look at the facts through the revisionist lens.

over and over again

She always found reasons not to leave her apartment, she did.

She became more and more nervous as doubts began to plague her.

She bitched and moaned about...

She danced until she could dance no more.

She had a dark side, an evil twist of the mind that frightened men.

She had a startling epiphany.

She rambled on and on about nothing.

She sighed audibly.

She was a "writer's writer."

She was truly paranoid. She honestly felt that everyone was out to get her.

Stupid is as stupid does.

The floorboards creaked and squeaked under his enormous weight. The proverbial elephant had entered the living room.

The itsy bitsy spider...

The room was sunny and bright.

The question as to whether...

The snow was whiter than white.

The sunset painted the sky orange.

They drove round and round in circles.

To reiterate:

To repeat:

To rephrase that,

To return to the topic,

Trained to be both gracious and polite, he seemed like the perfect gentleman.

up, up, and away

You can say that again.

WORD JUMBLE

Words like "truly" and "honestly" are fillers. Once in a blue moon, you can use them to add some style to your copy, but keep a meticulous watch on the "been there, done that" factor. In the example about the paranoid woman, the words *truly* and *honestly* make the two back-to-back sentences even more repetitive than they already are. Yes, they truly, honestly do. Really!

Keep It Simple Exercise: Meeting of the Minds

Write an email requesting a business meeting.

At the health club this afternoon, you talked to a man from your field that you had never met before. Happily, you exchanged business cards. Now you would like to befriend him as a networking contact, but you don't want to give him the impression that you're personally interested in him. Map out the email that you will send inviting him to a quick coffee at Starbucks. Take five minutes to figure out why he should agree to meet with you. Then, in short, declarative sentences, make your case. And, if this really *did* happen to you, type up your correspondence, girlfriend, and let it fly!

Keep It Simple Exercise Cheat Sheet: 5 Phrases to Experiment With

1. I would love to pick your brain about…
2. Let's kick-start the process by…
3. This, I promise:
4. Let's plan on…
5. Call me on my cell tomorrow.

And 1 Phrase to Avoid, No Matter What:

Or maybe we could just meet at a bar instead.

Section II:
Make It Provocative

You have two whole seconds to make an impression on a prospect. That's ⅕ of the length of a TV commercial. Even worse, your reader is holding a virtual remote control gadget in his hand, and he's got his finger on the button. After two seconds, he will either decide to stay with you or he will "zap" you forever. Whether you are writing a piece of direct mail copy, a brochure, or a resume, you will need to entice your readers from the beginning and never let them go. Start your message in the very first sentence!

There are five ways to make your copy provocative.

1. Be a Copy Tease. Ask Questions
2. Report News
3. Come Up with an Interesting Angle
4. Strike a Deal with Your Reader
5. Cite All Praise (But Sometimes, Be Humble About It)

We're over the two-second limit already, so before your attention span takes a stroll to the refrigerator...

1. Be a Copy Tease. Ask Questions

Every advertising siren knows that there's an art to seduction. Tantalize your readers from the very first sentence by prickling their curiosity and enticing them to learn more. Ask them questions about their hopes, fears, ambitions, and secret passions. Borrow heavily from the art of conversation and pepper your business letters with queries that engage your readers' hearts and minds. Why does asking a question work, you ask? Maybe it's because you're expressing interest in someone's life instead of endlessly jabbering about a product in client-speak. Hey, it's just a theory.

Are you happier today than you were four years ago?

Are you into chocolate martinis? Reading the Sunday *Times?*

Are you just an old-fashioned romantic?

Are you playing hide-and-seek with your creditors?

Are you stuck in the wrong career?

Are you working for a company that's about to go under?

Are you working too hard?

Can you trust the people who work for you?

Did you ever ask yourself...?

Did you ever notice...?

Do dogs resemble their owners after a while, or vice versa?

Do you enjoy looking at yourself? Or are you constantly checking your mirror for flaws?

Do you enjoy speaking in public? Or does getting in front of an audience make you break out in hives?

Do you ever dream of being self-employed?

Do you ever find yourself reminiscing about the good old days?

Do you ever wish that...?

Do you ever worry that your kids are growing up too fast?

Do you feel like you've achieved what you really want in life?

Do you let your dog sleep in your bed? Does your husband get jealous?

Do you like hip-hop? Or are you more into be-bop?*

Do you see the glass half-full or half-empty?

Do your kids like to play outdoors? Or are they always playing
   video games inside?

Does every woman have an inner goddess? Why is mine always on vacation?

Does she...or doesn't she? Hair color so natural only her hairdresser knows
for sure! (Clairol Tag Line)[1]

Fact or fiction? How do you know if the news you read
   in the papers is really true?

Has the Internet replaced TV? How many hours do you spend online every day?

Have you ever made a cold call? What happened?

How comfortable are you with today's technology?

How do you feel about helping your kids with their homework? Do you ever
secretly wish they'd just do it themselves?

How much money does it take to buy financial security?

How well do you really know your spouse?

If they can send a space shuttle to Mars, why can't they cure the common cold?

If you could change one feature on your face, what would it be?

If you were on a desert island, what three makeup items would you bring?

If your life were a book, what chapter would you be reading now?

In your opinion, who was the greatest female writer of the nineteenth century?

Is it harder to ask a male boss for a raise or a female boss?

Is it more important to be lucky or skillful?

Is one credit card *ever* enough?

Personal trainers, nutrition gurus, career coaches—necessities or perks of the privileged?

Ready to rekindle an old flame?

Remarkable, isn't it? How does the _____ Party get away with it?

The bigger the reward, the bigger the risk. But have you ever wondered...?

What does your office décor reveal about your personality?

What's your favorite color?

What's your opinion of the dating scene in Manhattan?

Where do you draw the line?

Why do teachers get paid so little money when their work is so important?

Would you ever go see a movie by yourself?

Writers need emotional support. But are writer chat groups really the best place to find it?

*For more "Genres," check out the Appendix.

Word Up
You can ask your prospect any question you like. But if it's a "yes" or "no" question, make sure that he will answer it the way that you intend. Okay?

[1] *Courtesy of Clairol/P&G ER NA Retail Haircolor*

2. Report News

Did you hear the latest? Starting a piece of copy with news adds a sense of urgency to your message. It's hot off the press, urging your readers to respond quickly. The news can be good or bad as long as it's hard-hitting (and factual). Sometimes, the grapevine can even yield fruit for thought, although you'll need to dish the dish quickly to avoid having your reader's interest shrivel up like a raisin in the sun. News often has a surprisingly short shelf life, and before you know it, there's mold forming along the edges. Keep your news fresh-squeezed. Be certain to fact check your copy nanoseconds before you let it loose over the transom. And in late-breaking developments...

A New Wrinkle in Time: Renowned Scientist Goes Back to
   the Future in the Present
According to PAGE SIX,
Airport security tightens as open-toed sandals hit the runways en masse
Brown bear spotted in mall. Shoppers ogle
Celebrities, from _____ to _____, swear by *The Jersey Shore Diet.*
Chemistry 101: New book argues that a hormone makes people feel like
   they're in love, even when they're not
Coming up next: school teachers revolt against cafeteria food.
Devastated Democrats force recount in Florida
Fighting the good fight: Hollywood takes on piracy
Five strangers caught in dragnet
Green tea may prevent certain types of cancer.
Gridlock alert: The president is in town. Expect traffic tie-ups in
   midtown after 3 p.m.
He's been spotted courting voters from Arkansas to Milwaukee.

I don't know if you caught the article in the *Times,* so I am sending it to you...
I heard through the grapevine...
I ran into our mutual friend Arthur Prescott last week, and he told me...
I was shocked and dismayed to hear...
In a recent survey,
In the past five years, hundreds of CEO jobs were downsized.
Is there life on Mars? 2007 mission probes for signs on Red Planet
Latchkey kids inspire new after-school program
Listening to upbeat music for just ten minutes a day can...
Logos are beyond in. Spotted on the runways from Milan to Paris...
More help wanted: Stores encourage seniors to apply for jobs
Nationwide poll shows support for war weakening
One million wait in line to view pope
One sniff of the male hormone androgen makes women feel calmer, happier,
   and more confident.
Political fallout: Mayor quits after scandal erupts
President's Report Card: More B's Than A's During His Second Term
Researchers suspect that a condition called "hypomania" is characterized by
a mental energy that is less intense than a manic frenzy.
"Retire split screens," jaded TV watchers implore network affiliates
Revivals take center stage on Broadway for second year in a row
Scientists discover paw print of first wooly mammoth
Stock prices reflect investor jitters
Supersize me: Giant sunglasses mask celebrities and celeb wanna-bes
Take this job and shove it: More Americans quit voluntarily

Teenagers call it "hooking up." And it means anything from making out to
   having sex.

The results from our nationwide survey are in...

The show, *Sex in the Suburbs,* is the network's first hit in...

The stock market dipped thirty points today, setting off fears that...

Thirty-six percent of smokers in Manhattan claim they smoke less now due
   to New York's smoking ban.

Top ten movie box office hits

"Twenty-five percent of the collection is fake," the museum's new
   director declared.

Two drinks, once a week, have been shown to...

Two elephants escaped from the parade yesterday.

Weak dollar drives tourists to the U.S. in droves

Where's the happiest place to live? Texas...and boy, are we glad you asked.

Winds of change at the Met

With two Golden Globe nominations, the movie is a definite Oscar contender.

Word Up

For every rule there is an exception, and one exception to the rule about making sure that your news is fresh is when you are dealing with a nostalgic topic. Writing a radio promotion for an oldies station? It's perfectly appropriate to flash with "news" that's really ancient history, such as, "On this day back in 1956, Elvis's smash single 'Don't Be Cruel' first hit the airwaves."

3. Come Up with an Interesting Angle

What do you do if your product is having a slow news month? In the absence of real news, you will need to come up with an intriguing angle—a few choice words that capture your product's benefits or personality in a way that prospects will relate to. In advertising circles, this little piece of magical language is often referred to as "positioning." But whether you call it an "angle," a "position," "the core message," or "a simple way in, damn it!" the language that you create needs to be true to the product for it to work. Here are some fantastic examples of the poetry of positioning.

Approach love and cooking with reckless abandon.

"Ask not what your country can do for you; ask what you can do for your country." (John F. Kennedy Inaugural Address)

Coincidence? We don't think so.

Confidential:

Contents require immediate attention:

Dating For Dummies (book by Dr. Joy Browne)

Don't give, tell. Don't grovel, sell.

Don't Look in the Basement (movie)

"Don't tell anyone, but..."

"Even a thousand-mile journey starts with a single step." (*Tao Te Ching,* book by Lao Tzu)

"Every woman needs a room of her own." (Virginia Woolf)

Fake pearls are better than the real thing. You never have to worry about them being stolen.

famous brands from around the world

Fashion is fickle. But true style is timeless.

Fashionistas have flocked to these flat moccasins with ornate beading.

First, learn the rules so that you'll know how to break them properly.

"Follow your bliss." (Joseph Campbell)

For millions of Americans, canned soup is the closest thing they ever have to a home-cooked meal.

girl power

Gorgeous, wealthy, and straight... There must be something wrong with him!

Has Internet dating lowered the moral bar?

He was a real superhero in his own mind.

"I find that the harder I work, the more luck I seem to have." (Thomas Jefferson)

"I may disagree with what you have to say, but I shall defend, to the death, your right to say it." (Voltaire)

If he isn't smart, how did he get to be so rich?

Ignorance is bliss.

In just thirty days, you can have your home business up and running.

In the '80s they were called "yuppies." But the yuppies objected, and today...

It Seemed Like a Good Idea at the Time (movie)

It was a mama cow of a suitcase.

It's like therapy without the $125 price tag.

Let's be honest,

Life is uncertain. Eat dessert first.

Lunch for Under $2? Clothing for Pennies? How to Do *Everything* Cheaper

luxe Italian tees

Married men live five years longer than single men, assuming their wives don't drive them crazy.

Most companies expect you to pay your dues for a couple of years. But here at _____,

Most of us grew up believing that one could never be too rich or too thin. But for millions of anorexic teenagers,

Most women turn into their mothers; few ever want to.

Night of the Living Dead (movie)

"One hand washes the other." (Petronius)

Our items never go on sale because our everyday prices are low.

Paradise. Just two hours from Manhattan, and less than a trip to Norwalk

People with pets are happier than people in pet-free households.

Pretty girls in bikinis are a marketer's dream. But...

Real Men Don't Eat Quiche (book by Bruce Feirstein and Lee Lorenz)

Seniors tend to be late adapters. So we invented...

She couldn't tell if it was love or merely an addiction.

She was charming to her acquaintances. But her employees saw a different side of her every day.

She was the first supermodel.

So what if she's chubby? That just means there's more of her to love.

Some of the "junk food" out there is better for you than the food that's considered good for you.

Statistics lie.

The Age of Innocence (book by Edith Wharton)

The Beverly Hillbillies (TV show)

The Good, the Bad, and the Undecided

The grass is always greener on the other side.

The Little Shop of Horrors (movie)

"The medium is the message." (Marshall McLuhan)

The most attractive beards are well-groomed with a hint of unruliness.

The Taming of the Shrew (play by William Shakespeare)

The Tao of Flower Arranging

The writing's on the wall.

There are two sides to every story.

This Side of Paradise (book by F. Scott Fitzgerald)

Three things a man should never do:

To keep weight off permanently, you need to lose it slowly.

Turns teeth movie-star white

What did Julius Caesar, Napoleon Bonaparte, Thomas Jefferson, and Sigmund Freud have in common? Migraines!

What do editors really want?

White wine is less caloric than red, but red is better for you. Who knew?

"Yes, Virginia, there is a Santa Claus." (Response by Francis P. Church, posted in the *New York Sun*)

You'd be shocked to learn how some employees lash out at their bosses.

Young, healthy people in their early twenties never want to deal with life insurance.

4. Strike a Deal with Your Reader

Always remember, your reader has one thing on her mind: what's in it for her, her, her? While that may sound just a tad narcissistic, it's your task to embrace your reader's self-interest and appeal to it. Chances are, she won't object to being entertained. She has a sense of humor too, thank you very much! But could you also throw in some freebies while you're at it? After all, she spent all that time reading your copy! Reward her generously for her effort—and witness the miracle of metamorphosis as your reader transforms into a loyal customer. Offer her a deal that's so irresistible that she'd have to be crazy to refuse it.*

Apply today and earn 25,000 bonus miles.

Come to our free seminar. No pressure to enroll.**

Early bird special: Reserve before 6 p.m. tonight and save

Fifteen percent off your first purchase when you open a credit card at *Oliver's Emporium*

Free mic readings on Thursday nights. Get discovered!

I can teach you how to make any man fall in love with you.

I would love to take you out to lunch to pick your brain about...

If you can spare fifteen minutes to meet me this week, I promise to make it worth your while.

If you had bought a condo (in this development), you'd be home by now.

If you're like me, you've probably tried to quit smoking a thousand times. But what if I could promise that you would never start smoking again?

Learn how to speak French (without having the person you're talking to reply in English).

Let it all hang out. Come to the Fat Is Fabulous Vegas Weekend.

100 percent satisfaction guaranteed

Proven to reverse bone loss caused by osteoporosis

Reconnect with your childhood friends.

Rent a cottage in East Hampton this summer (and we'll throw in the beach pass for free).

Renting a limousine for the prom may be a stretch. But you'll remember the night for the rest of your life.

Retrace your family history. Go to Ireland

Return this volume free of charge.

Take as long as you need to pay for large purchases. You won't incur any interest charges.

Text "hip hop" to 12345 on your mobile phone for a cool ring tone.

Tuesday is Ladies' Night. First two drinks on the house

You can always return it, no questions asked.

You can look ten years younger without going under the knife.

You'll look so svelte, you won't even recognize yourself.

*For more ways to press readers' hot buttons, see "Welcome to Youtopia," in the Appendix.

**For more "Free Words," check out the Appendix.

WATCH YOUR LANGUAGE

If you write copy for a living, it's frequently better to mention any disclaimers in the body of your text rather than hiding them in the fine print. Studies show that consumers tend to read captions and asterisk copy first. If your product happens to reverse only 85 percent of the bone loss caused by osteoporosis, don't be shy about bringing it to your customer's attention. It's still a great fact. And being open about it will inspire trust (and prevent persnickety calls from your ad agency's legal department down the road).

5. Cite All Praise (But Sometimes, Be Humble About It)

If your product or service has won awards, received accolades in the trades, or has become newsworthy, by all means, mention it. But try to be tactful about it. Have you ever met a name-dropper in your circle? Chances are, you were impressed for about five whole seconds. After that, you probably felt slightly nauseous (in between bouts of envy). You are not alone. Statistics show that nine out of ten people despise the one out of ten who are braggarts! Avoid needless chest beating, lest your consumers beat a hasty path to their circular files with your copy in hand.

At the age of seven, he was considered a prodigy.
B.M.O.C. (Big Man On Campus)
Back by popular demand…
best-selling
Big Swinging Dick
blue-chip stocks
Blue ribbon winner in the jumping event, _____,
bulge-bracket firm
By the time she died, she was the richest woman in America.
Critics love his new work.
Death-defying, _____,
Experts can't tell the difference between freshwater pearls and ours.
Fashion insiders report…
Financial planning guru, _____,
Five diamond hotel
"Give it all up for the today's M.V.P., _____!"

Gold Standard

Hall of Famer, _____,

_____ has become a household name

He was a name on the door at one of Washington's most prestigious law firms.

He was a top ten NBA draft pick.

He was nominated for the MacArthur Award twice during his lifetime.

He was voted the "sexiest man alive under forty" by _____.

He won two James Beard awards.

He's been a One Show winner three times in the past five years.

He's the world's richest real estate developer.

highly-acclaimed

His play received rave reviews in the *New York Times.*

International playboy, _____,

It has been designated a historical landmark.

It's the talk of the town.

Most of the marquee names in show business end up doing a stint in Vegas.

one of the most charismatic speakers on tour

Over one million copies sold!

patent pending

Political consultants: _____'s secret weapon at the polls

Princeton University named a library after her.

Pulitzer Prize-winning author...

Radio host to the stars...

rainmaker

_____ received sensational word-of-mouth

received the coveted _____ prize

She graduated from Brown, magna cum laude.

She took Chicago by storm.

She was a force to be reckoned with, according to all four of her husbands.

She was featured in *PARADE* magazine.

She was mostly famous for being famous.

She was Stravinsky's muse.*

She was the darling of the _____ set.

She was voted "Most Likely to Succeed" by her graduating class.

She's a **boldface** on PAGE SIX.

She's a starlet from a famous acting family.

She's won literally every advertising award in the book.

Supermodel and IT-girl, _____,

Talk show mogul, _____,

The A-List

The crème de la crème**

The critics are unanimous. This is the Date Movie to see this summer!

The face that launched a thousand ships.

the inner circle

The *New York Times* once called her the "Networking Queen."

The #1 selling _____ in America

The paparazzi followed her everywhere.

The *Wall Street Journal* gave the film a star.

The youngest V.P. in the firm, _____,

This diva of daytime has thousands of fans.

_____ tops the worst-dressed list.

up-and-coming pop star sensation

Urban legend, _____,

Wine connoisseurs have noted its floral tones.***

won accolades

word-of-mouth sensation

world-famous

world-renowned

*For other "Words That Are Beyond Fabulous," check out the Appendix.

**For more "French Words That You Hear Bandied About," see Section V, 13.

***For "More Words from Our Distinguished Wine and Spirits Collection," check out the Appendix.

WORD JUMBLE

Be careful about using intensifiers like the word "literally." In the example here about the woman who won awards, it's doubtful that she won literally every single advertising award out there. There are at least ten of them, or thirty if you count bronze, silver, and gold. Did she win ten awards? Twenty? Thirty? Not knowing how many awards she won can literally make your readers climb the walls! (Of course, only superhero action figures in cute Spiderman outfits can *literally* climb walls.)

Make It Provocative Exercise: You at Your Most Magnificent

Write a personal ad to post on one of the popular Internet dating sites.

Come up with an intriguing angle, hook, or spin to give yourself. Are you gregarious or more introspective? Think about how to convey a snapshot of your personality without resorting to a bunch of hype that your reading audience will see right through. For example, you might start by citing a book that you've read recently or a movie that you watched where you identified with the main character. Set your timer. Give yourself exactly twenty-five minutes to write your personal ad. Then stop, and let it sit for an hour. After that, take fifteen minutes to fine-tune your masterpiece.

Make It Provocative Exercise Cheat Sheet: 5 Phrases to Experiment With

1. Marriage-minded wealthy doctor seeks…
2. I'm a virgin to the whole Internet dating scene.
3. Repentant divorcee desires second chance at love
4. Looking for a great stepmom for two adorable kids. (Mine)
5. Former Miss North Carolina seeks some southern comfort

And 1 Phrase to Avoid, No Matter What:

Sex dynamo seeks bedroom jock

Section III:
Nix the Bells and Whistles

With all due respect to Rice Krispies' charming tag line, the *Snap! Crackle! Pop!* school of advertising has seen its heyday, and passed it. Today, having too many bells and whistles in a piece of copy can take away the integrity of your message. (This doesn't mean that you can never use an exclamation point to underscore your point! Or a parenthesis.) But, as a general rule, have confidence that your ideas will convey the tone perfectly—especially when you are using humor.

There are five ways to nix the bells and whistles.

1. Don't Over Punctuate. Period
2. Stop Trying to Reinvent the Wheel. Master Those Pesky Grammar Rules Instead of Always Breaking Them
3. Eliminate All Transitions That Clank
4. Assume That Your Reader Is as Smart as You Are. No Two-by-Fours to the Forehead
5. Don't Point Out That You Just Made a Joke

Wait! Did you get the joke in the third sentence, the one that used the exclamation point?

1. Don't Over Punctuate. Period

In Adspeak, every joke comes with an exclamation point or an emoticon. It's almost as if the punctuation is attempting to function as a huge "Applause" sign (while the copywriter tries to direct the reader's reaction to his advertising copy). We may all wish to tell our reading audience to [insert laugh here]. But doing so seriously dumbs down our copy. Be honest: has the laugh track in a sitcom *ever* made you laugh when the writing was lame?

Try writing your solicitations in the King's English, rather than in Adspeak. And you'll sound like a king, rather than a mere copywriter.

Phrase...	Phrase, Correctly Punctuated, Becomes...
As if this weren't enough...	As if this weren't enough,
But wait!	But wait:
Buy two tickets to see the movie. Get the third ticket FREE!	Buy two tickets to see the movie. Get the third ticket free.
Buyer beware!	Buyer beware.
Concerts, theater, film festivals, and more!	Concerts, theater, film festivals, and more.
Congratulations, Marcia!	Congratulations, Marcia.
Dazzling!	Dazzling.
Experts may differ...	Experts may differ.
Help! My teacher just assigned an essay, and I can't figure out where to start! Do you have any ideas for me?????	Help. My teacher just assigned an essay, and I can't figure out where to start. Do you have any ideas for me?

If you are one of the two men
   who read my man-bashing novel...

Inside: Your sexy swimsuit finder!

Jilted Jennifer is mad as hell!

Last chance to save 30 percent!!!

P.S. Miss me already, don't you?☺

Show up before 11 a.m. and get
   your free goodie bag. Yay!

Sing! Dance! Act! in our summer
   Shakespeare festival.

Special issue!

Spring sale. Three days only!

Thanks, Mary!

Tired of battling lines at the casino?
   New handheld device lets you
   play 21 on your own time!*

With all due respect to the men
   in the audience...

You break it, you own it!

You can only guess the rest...

You'll always remember the
   first time...

You're crazy!

If you are one of the two men
   who read my man-bashing novel,

Inside: Your sexy swimsuit finder.

Jilted Jennifer is mad as hell.

Last chance to save 30 percent.

P.S. Miss me already, don't you?

Show up before 11 a.m. and get
   your free goodie bag.

Sing, dance, act in our summer
   Shakespeare festival.

Special issue.

Spring sale. Three days only.

Thanks, Mary.

Tired of battling lines at the casino?
   New handheld device lets you
   play 21 on your own time.

With all due respect to the men
   in the audience,

You break it, you own it.

You can only guess the rest.

You'll always remember the
   first time.

You're crazy.

---

*For more "You Will Be Modern and in Vogue" words, see Section IV, 3.

{ LANGUAGE POLICE
There are very few times when you really need to use an ellipsis, but for some strange reason…the humble ellipsis constantly crops up in Adspeak. Don't go there. As David Ogilvy once wrote, "The consumer isn't a moron. She's your wife." (And presumably, you married her because she was smart and not an arm ornament.) }

2. Stop Trying to Reinvent the Wheel. Master Those Pesky Grammar Rules Instead of Always Breaking Them

There's no need to be comma-phobic. Still, the common comma inspires fear in many writers who can't decide whether or not to commit to them. The rule is simple. But it's been broken so many times by *journalists* that now all of the other writers out there—copywriters, promotion writers, screenwriters, and novelists—are scratching their heads in complete confusion. (Leave it to a whole subset of writers to unilaterally decide to drop certain commas just to save space!) Please separate all lists by commas—unless you're a journalist, in which case you get a free press pass to bypass the comma before the last word in the list.

baked potatoes, peanut oil, salt, garlic powder, sugar, silicon dioxide

Bali is an Indonesian island that's known for its lavish dances, rituals, and handcrafted artworks.

Dante, Boccaccio, Botticelli, and Raphael were all born in Florence.*

"Early to rise and early to bed / Makes a man healthy, wealthy, and dead." (Ogden Nash)

Essential wardrobe items: three skirts, three sweaters, one jacket, and five pairs of shoes.

Fight cellulite, flab, and jiggle.

Fireworks cancelled on Main Beach over July 4th weekend. Hot dog, apple
pie, and beer sales unaffected.

Good reviews, positive word-of-mouth, and the ability to create a stir will
turn any product into a smash success.

He survived tuberculosis, meningitis, and colon cancer, only to die in his sleep.

He was blond-haired, strong, and silent. Even better, he was straight!

He was friendly to neighbors, dogs, and policemen. There's no way that he
could be an ax murderer!

Her eyebrows had been tweezed, arched, and penciled in to express
continual surprise.

His eyes were blue, blue-green, gray, or hazel depending on his mood.

His lyrics inspired fiction writers, poets, and budding songwriters throughout the
U.S.

"I came, I saw, I conquered." (Julius Caesar)

"I have nothing to offer but blood, toil, tears, and sweat." (Winston Churchill)

If you roll a two, three, or twelve on your first throw, it's called "craps."

It's important to eat from the four food groups—peanuts, popcorn, pretzels,
and potato chips.

It's the movie with the most thrills per minute, the most stunning special
effects, and the most realistic acting.

"Let's group ourselves alphabetically: A–M, please stand over here; N–R,
take the center; S–Z, stand in the corner."

Martin Luther, John Calvin, and John Knox were three leaders of the Reformation.

Monkeys, lions, tigers, bears, and zebras coexist peacefully at the Bronx Zoo.

Most women shorter than 5'2" enjoy wearing one-inch, two-inch, or three-inch heels.

Multi-vitamin tablets usually include vitamins A, C, E, and various forms of B.

One potato, two potatoes, three potatoes, four.

One small red onion, sliced, marinated, and separated into rings

Orange juice, carrots, and peaches: it's the all-orange diet.**

Prepositions such as "up," "of," and "into" weigh down strong verbs and bring copy to a grinding halt.

reading, writing, and arithmetic

ready, willing, and able

red, white, and blue

Sautéing beef, peppers, and onions in cilantro for fifteen minutes gives them a pungent kick.

Seductive hair: sexy, long, and healthy.

Sex, Lies, and Videotape (movie)

Shopping list: eggs, bread, soda, frozen waffles, and ice cream.

Spending long periods of time in an isolation tank could cause hallucinations, anxiety, and severe depression.

strong, sturdy, and made of 100 percent scratch-resistant plastic

tall, dark, and handsome

"The approach to style is by way of plainness, simplicity, orderliness, sincerity." (*The Elements of Style,* book by William J. Strunk Jr. and E. B. White)

"The beautiful part of writing is that you don't have to get it right the first time, unlike, say, a brain surgeon." (Robert Cormier)

The Lion, the Witch, and the Wardrobe (book by C. S. Lewis)

The powerful CEO was used to being respected, feared, and just plain
    despised.
There are always three groups of people to whom you're writing:
    the innovators, the early adopters, and the laggards.
Tom, Dick, and Harriet
Victory formula: carb up, rest up, and after a setback, chin up.
What are the four most popular pizza toppings? Mushrooms, onions,
    pepperoni, and anchovies, of course!
What are the three most important things in real estate? Location, location,
    location.
"When angry, count to ten before you speak; if very angry, a hundred."
    (Thomas Jefferson)***
Will wash floors, windows, and tubs. Won't do toilets.
Witness the seven wonders of the ancient world: the Colossus of Rhodes,
    the Hanging Gardens of Babylon, the Pharos of Alexandria, the Pyramids
    of Egypt, the Statue of Jupiter by Phidias, the Temple of Diana at
    Ephesus, and the Tomb of Mausolus.

*For more "Artsy Words," check out the Appendix.
**For a list of "Colors," including the color orange, check out the Appendix.
***See "Numbers, Weights, and Measurements," Section V, 11.

> **Word Up**
> Consistency may be the "hobgoblin of little minds," but when it comes to writing copy, it's far better to *consistently* break a grammar rule than to respect it only occasionally. Readers will get confused and lose confidence in your ability to relay information. So if you insist on dropping the last comma in the list, please be certain to drop it every single time (and pray that no grammarians write you long, caustic letters with every comma perfectly in place!).

3. Eliminate All Transitions That Clank

You need transitions. But if every paragraph that you write begins with a transition, your copy will sound like a school teacher wrote it—a scholastic exercise in futility for all but the most professorial. The list of conceivable transitions is long and ungainly. Use them, but use discretion. See if your ideas will hold together without transitions, and eliminate all but the essential ones. If you're new at the writing game, run your copy by a pro before letting it fly. (By "pro" we do not mean to infer someone who writes infomercial copy for knife sets airing at three in the morning on some station that you've never heard of—not that there's anything wrong with that!)

Additionally,

All things considered,

Along these lines,

Also, let's not forget...

And, in the end, we must ask ourselves if...

And, just for calling in today, we'll give you...

And so it seems,

And that's not all,

As an added bonus,

As if that's not enough, we'll also throw in...

As of this minute,

As to whether

As yet

At the same time,

Believe it or not,

Besides which,

Best of all,

But look at the bright side:

But there's even more.

Considering the fact that...

Crazy, isn't it?

Currently, the feeling is...

During the time that...

Fairly recently,

Finally,

First off,

For more information about,

For starters,

Furthermore,

He could not help but...

He is regarded as being...

He was a man who...

Her side of the story went
   something like this:

Importantly,

In conclusion,

In a nutshell,

In many cases,

In point of fact,

In regard to

In short,

In sum,

In terms of

In the event of...

In the final analysis,

In the not-so-distant past,

Inside of

It certainly seemed to suggest...

It wasn't just

Many times,

Meanwhile,

No wonder...

Normally, this knife set would retail
for $19.95. But if you take advantage
of this special offer...

One of the most interesting
   improvements has been...

Personally,

Plus,

Presently,

Regarding,

Regrettably,

Sad to say, but...

Secondly,

So far,

So for the foreseeable future,

Still,

That was a great point,
  no doubt, but...

Thanking you in advance for your
    attention to this matter,

The thrust of his argument was...

The truth is,

Thirdly,

To begin with,

To summarize,

We're certain that you'll agree...

What's more,

Will you indulge me here
  for a second?

With some difficulty, she said
  the following:

You'll also be surprised to discover,

WATCH YOUR LANGUAGE

Every piece of writing that you create needs a structure, but you don't want the structural underpinnings to show. (This is the grammatical equivalent of flashing your lingerie in public—something you shouldn't do often unless you're a female rock star with amazing abs.) Glance at your copy. If you see a lot of words there like "First," "Second," and "Finally," it's time to lift and tighten your sentence structure. Good, strong supporting points hold up a piece of copy seamlessly, without a lot of rhetorical padding.

4. Assume That Your Reader Is as Smart as You Are. No Two-by-Fours to the Forehead

Even very seasoned writers often succumb to the "carrot stick" school of copywriting. They make a promise in the first paragraph that they threaten to take away in the last paragraph. This isn't just oily, it's positively slick—a shining moment for hucksters. And you wonder why advertising consistently ranks as one of the "least trusted" professions and why most people unceremoniously toss out their direct mail without even bothering to open it! Every piece of copy needs to have integrity. Don't include a deadline unless it's real. (Hint: The offer really must expire for the deadline to be considered real.)

Don't Promise...	Only to Take It Back...
"After"	All "Before" shots were taken without any makeup.
All-you-can-eat buffet!	As long as you don't exceed the three-plate maximum.
As a preferred customer,	But act now, before our rates go up.
As the president of the firm, I will personally handle your account.	My junior account executive, Stanley, will be calling you to set up breakfast.
Bring this postcard to the counter for a tote bag, absolutely free.	With every purchase of $30 or more.
Buy tickets over the phone to avoid long lines at the box office.	There may be a short line at the automated ticket dispenser.
Check out these chic (and cheap) fabulous finds!	T-shirt, $9; jeans, $20; bandanna, $2; shoes, $730.

Cowboy boots now available in every skin.

Except for ostrich, shark, and lizard.

Each frozen cappuccino drink has a double shot of espresso to give you the energy you need to succeed.

Has been known to make some people jittery. Do not drive a car afterwards or operate heavy machinery.

Electrolysis kills the hair follicle so no hair will ever grow back in the pore that was zapped.

Now you only need to deal with the other one million hair follicles on the surface of your face.

Enroll now in our beginner writer's workshop.

Writing sample required.

Every contribution counts, no matter how small.

Would you consider a starter gift of $1,000?

Fewer roaming charges with our new national plan

And only fifty fewer free minutes a month!

Free cup of coffee and biscotti...

When you fill out our completely objective "tell us how we're doing" survey.

Free downloaded tunes...

With three proof of purchase stickers.

Free hologram bookmark

If you simply punch in your email address.

Free makeover...

When you purchase two products of $30 or more.

Free spa lunch...

Free support group meetings...

Free V.I.P. passes for the first fifty
people to log on...
Genuine designer handbags at 80
percent off.
Get a two-bedroom apartment for the
price of a one-bedroom
Go whaling!

_____ has been proven to protect against
sixteen visible signs of aging.
"I lost fifty pounds in just five weeks!"
I would like to personally welcome
you to the club.
I'm just writing to personally thank you
for being a leader of the class.
to donate $2,000 more than
In just twelve classes, you'll learn how
to take charge of your own finances
so that you won't have to depend
on anyone to do it for you.

When you sign up for $255 of our
salon services.
Once you sign up for our seven-
day-a-week food plan.
With a subscription to _____
magazine.
Seconds, irregulars, and slightly
used...All look brand new!
Second bedroom is windowless.

After five hours, if there are no
whales, the boat will turn
around and go back to shore.
According to all six of the the
subjects in our study.*
Individual results vary.**
Call 1-800-123-4567 and ask to
speak to Operator 61.
With your tenth reunion around
the corner, may I encourage you
you did last year?
The instructor of the class,
_____, is a financial planner
with over twenty years of
experience. He is available
for paid consultations.

It's a word-for-word remake of the original.

Except that the main character has been changed from a man to a woman.

It's sugar-free, with zero carbs.

Only four hundred eighty calories per serving.

It's the movie version of the book you love.

Now with songs and dances!

Karaoke set, 50 percent off!

Songs sold separately.

Laser surgery gives you perfect vision.

You will still need to wear reading glasses.

Learn to surf fish the Narragansett Bay in one easy lesson

Must have previous experience.

Makes age spots disappear instantly!

Be certain to wear sunscreen of SPF 45 or higher and stay out of the sun!

No pressure.

A personal representative will call you at your convenience.

No salesmen will call.

Simply fill out the survey and your daytime phone number to get started.

No strings.

Please review our detailed Consent Agreement and check off that you have read it.

Nobody beats our prices

Just bring in an ad from one of our competitors and we'll be happy to match their price.

Open every day, from 10 a.m. to 5 p.m.

Our high-tech bra lifts and separates naturally

Peels away the dead skin to reveal the fresher skin underneath.

Please donate $25 right away to keep programs like this on the air.

Proven to grow new hair

Renovating? Rent an apartment with all of the amenities of home.

Salon styling gels, deeply discounted

Sign up now and you'll win a free ice-pink lipstick!

Sit back and relax in our casual family eatery.

60 percent-off sale going on now!

Except Fridays, Saturdays, and Sundays.

Most women don't even feel the underwire or silicon-filled sacks.

After a six-week trial period, if you're not totally satisfied, you can always return the unused portion for a full refund.

After our (four-hour) telethon.

For as long as you keep using our product. If you ever stop using our formula, your new hair will fall out.

Phone service, extra. Internet connection, extra. Garbage pick up, extra.

To be certain your product is authentic, please buy it in the salon.

As long as supplies last.

Dress code: no jeans, sneakers, or open-toed sandals.

Consult individual stores for details.

Suppresses your appetite for
twelve hours.

The most livable apartments in the city!

THE SALE

The world's largest collection of
hand-woven Oriental rugs

The world's most intelligent smoke
filter

There are three spots open in our
kindergarten class!

These handcrafted sweaters are made
to last forever.

This book will teach anyone how to
draw lifelike figures and objects.

This commercial-free rock hour...

This sturdy porch umbrella stands up to
winds of 60 mph.

Trade in your miles for a free domestic
trip anywhere in the U.S.

Waterproof mascara

We're just happy to welcome you.

Win $1,000 in the next few minutes.

If you don't see results after up to
three weeks, consult a physician.

Sign up now to get on our two-
year wait list!

Up to 10 percent off selected items.

Some may be machine-crafted.

Must keep machine at least two
feet away from walls and furniture.

Not including legacies.

A special warranty guarantees
them for ten years.

You can always supplement your
learning with our $470 seminar.

has been sponsored by...

Keep porch umbrella closed during
a rainstorm.

Except during holidays, weekends,
and other high-volume
periods during the year.

Washes off easily!

As a new member, would you
consider a special gift?

All you have to do is be our six-
teenth caller.

With the right equipment, it's easy to catch blue claw crabs.

Year-end blockbuster whites sale!
You have been pre-approved…
You have been specially selected…
You have won a free trip to Hawaii!

You will receive a stroke of good fortune in the next three days.

You'll receive our magazine absolutely free.
Your thighs will lose that "orange peel" look practically overnight.

You're on the "short list" to be included in our special volume of important professionals.
You're one of the very few people to whom I am writing today.
Yours for only $29.95.

And, as long as the crabs measure five inches from point to point, you can even keep them!
Linens and towels not included.
This offer expires on 6/14.
As long as your credit history…
Just be sure to visit our beautiful time-share properties.
But you must forward this email to fourteen of your closest friends. Do not break the chain or bad luck will follow!
Simply apply your frequent flyer miles towards it.
After just twenty weekly appoint-ments you'll start to notice a real difference.
Please fill out the enclosed application and include the $70 processing fee.
There's only one spot left in the seminar! Call immediately.
You simply agree to buy at least six books a year from our catalogue!

---

*For more "Isn't She Lovely? Beauty Words," check out the Appendix.
**For more "Words to Diet for," check out the Appendix.

Word Up
Stop faking it. Consumers today are marketing savvy. Haven't we all received numerous solicitations for magazines at 50 percent off the newsstand price long *after* the deadline supposedly expired? Before you include a fake deadline, think about how you react to them. And just for good measure, reread that lovely children's story, "The Boy Who Cried Wolf." Today, you're going to have to be a lot cleverer about how you approach your customers if you want them to take you seriously.

---

5. Don't Point Out That You Just Made a Joke

If you have to explain that you just made a joke, it's probably not all that hilarious. But, just like in stand-up comedy, having confidence in your wit takes some practice. Is your copy as funny as you think it is? One way to find out is to let it gestate for a couple of days after you write it. Then, reread it. Does it make you laugh out loud? If it doesn't, it's not funny enough (calling for a serious rewrite). Avoid phrases that take the edge off your writing by winking at the reader, or enclosing phrases that are supposed to be taken ironically in quotation marks.

A cartoon light bulb went off in his head.

And the punch line is...

But all fooling aside,

But seriously...

But the twist is:

"But you already know that I think that your sister's pretty," he said, putting his foot in his mouth for the third time that night.

Can you believe it?

Cracking a smile, she said...

Did you hear the one about the guy who...?

Drum roll, please...

Funny,

Get it?

Get out of here!

Guess you had to be there.

He lampooned the fraternity practice of hazing its newest members.

_____, he said, ever the straight man.

_____, he said, ever the wag.

_____, he said, tongue-in-cheek.

He was a "rock star," if only in his own mind.

He was so humorless that just seeing his dour, frowning face made her giggle.

"Hello, Todd. To what do I owe this pleasure?" she said sarcastically.

Her antics made me crack up.

Her laugh, a cross between a blue jay's tweet and a woodpecker's drill, made us chortle right along with her.

Her wit could be lethal. Tonight's opening salvo was no exception.

His rollicking banter normally put his guests at ease. Except when they found themselves to be the butt-end of his jokes.

If she's really "married to her job," how come her husband doesn't ever get jealous?

If the film doesn't make you laugh out loud, it's probably because you had a lobotomy recently and haven't fully recuperated.

Ironically,

It was a laugh riot.

It was several weeks before I could see any humor in the situation.

"It won't be white, that's for sure," snipped a guest at Mary's fourth wedding.

No one took the news of the sultan's marriage to his longtime mistress with a straight face. Even his wife didn't blink an eye.

Say it isn't so!

She laughed hysterically.

She looks like she's had some work done. Meow!

_____, she said, jokingly.

_____, she said, returning his witty banter.

_____, she said, with a conspiratorial wink at her nemesis.

_____, she said, with self-deprecating charm.

She was a brunette until she turned forty. After that she was suddenly "blonde."

She was a poor little rich girl, a "princess" who grew up in the kingdom of East Orange, New Jersey.

Some quote, unquote "antiques…"

Surely, you jest.

the new job "security"

The way that she laughed out loud at her own jokes was far more humorous than the jokes themselves. We had no choice but to be a good audience.

We both laughed out loud.

We started rolling in the aisles with laughter.

What a laugh!

wink-wink, nudge-nudge

You can't be serious!

{ **WORD JUMBLE**
One drawback of using quotation marks to point out your jokes is that it's hard to figure out when to stop using them. In the joke about the poor little rich girl, if the word princess is in quotes, then shouldn't the word kingdom also be in quotes? But, if you put the word kingdom in quotes, the whole sentence falls flat, eliminating the need for quotation marks in the first place. }

Nix the Bells and Whistles Exercises:

The following two exercises will help you master different skills. The first writing assignment will help you brush up on your grammar, while the second one will help you become more adept at humorous writing.

CEO Material

Write an email to get out of going to the office Christmas party.

The mercurial CEO at your office has cordially demanded that every single employee attend the office Christmas party on December 18. The problem is that your birthday happens to fall on December 18 and weeks before you heard a word about an office party, you organized a dinner on that night for ten of your closest friends. Take thirty minutes to craft the email that you will send to your boss's boss's boss, politely explaining why you can't attend the office party. First, come up with the official reason that you will provide for your absence. Then write your RSVP in a way that proves you're both a team player and a stellar employee worth keeping around.

Nix the Bells and Whistles Exercise I Cheat Sheet: 5 Phrases to Experiment With

1. Unfortunately, my mother-in-law is going to be staying with us that night.
2. I was quite upset to learn that my wife is going to be out of town, and I have baby-sitting responsibilities.

3. I will be getting root canal surgery that afternoon, and my dentist has advised…

4. I was really looking forward to the office party. But my wife is nine months pregnant, and…

5. I have a wedding to attend that day—my own!

And 1 Phrase to Avoid, No Matter What:

I will be entertaining clients after 6 p.m., and so… (Probably, you could just invite them to the office party!)

The Accidental Toastmaster

Write a marriage toast.

In a few short weeks, your best friend on the planet will get hitched. That's the good news. The bad news is that he has elected you to give the toast, and you're terrified to speak in public. Try to inject some humor into your toast without turning it into vicious roast. Also, resist the urge to point out when you've made a joke. Think in terms of structure. How did the amorous couple first meet? Did their relationship take off instantaneously, or did you have to play Dear Abby a few times? Take thirty-five minutes and write out your speech. Then, let your speech gestate overnight, and tackle it again tomorrow with fresh eyes.

Nix the Bells and Whistles Exercise II Cheat Sheet: 5 Phrases to Experiment With

1. "It was love at first sight; well, on Pete's side, it was."
2. "Fortunately, Petra ignored the advice of her sorority sisters, and…"
3. "I knew it was getting serious when Pete actually went out and bought a tie to wear. It was silk, too—not something he picked up at the 99-cents store."
4. "I worried that Petra would never forgive Pete for giving her a mouse pad for her birthday."
5. "Will you join me now and raise a glass to toast the happy couple?"

And 1 Phrase to Avoid, No Matter What:
"He was dating this girl named Laura at the time, and…"

Section IV:
Closing Arguments

In closing, you'd like to thank your mother for having you, your boss for hiring you, and your boyfriend for tolerating your addiction to halibut—except that you're never going to win any awards for your advertising copy unless you can nail those closing arguments! Eloquently rephrase your promise, but in language that is markedly different from your opening paragraph. Then, go back and make certain that your argument is airtight from the beginning of your copy to the end. After all, nobody respects an argument with loopholes.

There are five types of closing arguments.

1. Your Friends Will Writhe with Envy
2. For Richer or Richer
3. You Will Be Modern and in Vogue
4. You Will Achieve Peace of Mind
5. Sex Appeal

Don't flip-flop (or argue with yourself endlessly) about what your closing argument should be. Just pick a direction and argue the heck out of it.

1. Your Friends Will Writhe with Envy

Back in the 1950s, a lot of marketers urged their customers to "keep up with the Joneses." But today, if you're only keeping up, you're falling behind. Most marketers worth their salt will still encourage you to compare your lifestyle to your neighbor's. But while "thou shall not covet thy neighbor's wife," these days, hopefully your neighbor will covet your wife's car! Pushing the envy button may sound Machiavellian, but it works. Promise your prospects that they will make the Joneses jealous as hell.

"Don't tell me I'm not the greatest. I'm the double greatest." (Muhammad Ali)

Even his rivals call him "King Solomon," a testament to his ability to solve complex business problems.

French Women Don't Get Fat (book by Mireille Guiliano)

Friends don't let friends poach their boyfriends.

Go ahead. Let your neighbors think you're having a mid-life crisis. A little red _____ will make a stunning addition to your driveway.

How can she possibly afford that, friends may titter.

"How did she get that St. Bart's tan?" (They'll never know it came from a bottle)

How one family's lawn turned a whole neighborhood green with envy

"I guess I'm just lucky," she said. "My metabolism has always been really fast."

Invite your friends over to watch your favorite *Hang Out at the Hospital* episodes.

But keep an eye on your friends' reactions to your new flat screen TV. You don't want your own life to turn into a soap opera!

Makes jaws drop to the floor

Men adored her while women despised her.

"Mine is bigger," he said, pointing to his brand new SUV.

She always manages to snag the best-looking boyfriends, even though she's
nothing to write home about.

She was plump in all the right places, lips, breasts, and butt, and skinny in all the
right places, arms, legs, and stomach.

Tell everyone that you've been working out five times a week.

"That chick is toast!"

We can't all have hourglass figures. But we can dress as if we do.

"What, this old thing? Twenty bucks at a yard sale."

"When I first met Gary, I could only do two crunches. Now I can do fifty in a row."

With our stunning highlight kit, no one will ever guess that you did it yourself.

"You da man!"*

You don't have to be a Society dowager to throw a world-class bash.**

Your friends may ask if there's a new man in your life. After all, you never had
that glow before.

You're never too old to master bridge. And once you do, you'll be in demand
every night of the week.

---

*For more words "From the 'Hood," see Section V, 13.
**For more "Festive Words," see Section V, 5.

{ **WATCH YOUR LANGUAGE**
While jealousy is one coveted reaction, sometimes the thing that you're really after is "word of mouth" advertising, where you'll need to encourage your customer to share information with her friends and neighbors (instead of always keeping them in the dark). Need a reality check? Run your "strategy" by a couple of sage marketing gurus before letting your copy rip. (Don't know any gurus? Write to vicky@vickyoliver.com) }

2. For Richer or Richer

If anyone ever tells you it's about the principle, it's always about the money. So one smart principle of classic marketing is to "show him the money." Tell your prospect how he will save it, make it, manage it, double it, park it, rake it in, roll it over, sit on it, grow it into a nest egg, borrow against it, lend it, or even leave it to his heirs. Unless he's King Tut, your potential customer already knows that he can't take it with him. So how can you help your target enjoy more of the green stuff in the here and now?

Are you a spendthrift? Hoarder? Financial Luddite? Learn how to amass money in spite of your financial personality type.

At _____, free checking really is free. What a concept.

Death and taxes are the only sure things. But at _____, taxes needn't...

Do the fabulously rich see opportunities that elude others? Or are they given more opportunities to begin with?

F. Scott Fitzgerald once wrote, "The rich are different than you and I."

Financial institutions vs. the little guy: Why Goliath always triumphs

Freakonomics: A Rogue Economist Explores the Hidden Side of Everything (book by Steven D. Levitt and Stephen J. Dubner)

Free checking vs. a free toaster. You decide.

Friends and family save 30 percent. Loyalty has its rewards

Full house. Vegas strikes back at card counters

Haven't you squandered enough money on ponchos that you never end up wearing?

How to Avoid Getting Gouged at the Pump This Summer

Imagine having two gorgeous_____ for the price of one.

It has the identical software as name-brand computers, but it's far less costly.

July is employee discount (for everyone) month

Let's Make a Deal (TV show)

Lifestyles of the Rich and Famous (TV show)

Million dollar babies. Prices of Manhattan apartments climb higher, despite fears
   of real estate "bubble"

Money talks.

Most couples only fight about three things: money, money, and money.

Now that pre-washed jeans boast designer prices, denim-wearers break them in
   the old-fashioned way.

Old money vs. new money. What a difference a few generations can make

Our combined buying power guarantees that you'll get the lowest price.

Our laptop may not be a fashion statement. But it works.

Play the stock market without losing your shirt, car, house (or dignity).

Pre-owned, a vintage classic

safety net

Smart Women Don't Let Dummies Handle Their Money

Take advantage of the fact that the dollar is so low. Come visit the U.S.

That's just too steep a price to pay!

The biggest risk is taking none at all.

"The check is in the mail."

The first million is the hardest.

The higher the risk, the higher the reward. But...

The Price Is Right (TV show)

The Reversible Mortgage. It turns everything you ever knew about mortgages upside down

The rich keep getting richer. But what about the rest of us?

The $64,000 Question (TV show)

Trust fund babies—are they just spoiled rich kids?

Weightless makeup. Without the prices that cause frown lines

Who Wants to Be a Millionaire? (TV show)

Why pay a stockbroker when you can have access to the exact same research he uses?

Why should the middle class have to pay more taxes than this country's wealthiest citizens?

Winter cruise to Alaska

You can spend a little more now or a lot more later. The choice is yours.

You get what you pay for.

You work hard for your money. But is your money working hard enough for you?

You'll save more than you spend. Even your spouse can't object to that.

You're so close to taking the next big step in your life. Perhaps you've always dreamed of upgrading to a bigger home. Or putting a down payment on your first country house.

You're worth it.

3. You Will Be Modern and in Vogue

High-tech gadgets morph in nanoseconds, and suddenly yesterday's Palm Pilot must be replaced. The good news is that people who enjoy gadgets also like to update them constantly. These techies are hard-wired to adapt to the times and eager to learn about the next "new new thing." In real time (and real dollars), these geeks of chic may be your best customers. Sometimes the demand for great innovations even outpaces the supply. You don't really have to sell new toys to the boys. You're simply informing them about what's out there.

aerodynamic styling cuts wind resistance

blog

Business @ the Speed of Thought (book by Bill Gates)

Cordless, so you can keep your hands on the wheel (and your eyes on the road).

Change is good

Change is the only constant.

Chat with your friends in "real time."

digitized for truer sound

e-commerce

electroplated for indestructibility

ergonomically designed to support your back

Fly the beautiful skies of your living room with our radio-controlled mini 747.

Futurama (TV show)

futuristic designs

German-engineered

green machines

Hybrid power trains run quieter than traditional engines.*

In a nation of gas-guzzlers, hybrids pull ahead*

India poised to export the $100 computer to the five billion people worldwide
   who still don't have Internet access.

It keeps your finger on the pulse.

It's like having your own personal MIS guy.

Laser away hair painlessly and permanently.

Laser light show with surround-sound technology.

Learn how to fly a rocket ship with our Flight Simulator software.

Life discovered on Mars

life in the pod

M.V.N.O.'s (Mobile Virtual Network Operators) launch video games on cells

Major studios prepare to let movie watchers download films legally man the controls

On Monday night, you'll have a choice of three endings. Vote for your favorite.

on the cusp

on the cutting edge

on the cutting room floor

on the leading edge

One of the most phenomenal peripheral makers out there will soon be moving
into the _____ market.

one remote to program all your remotes

Our point and shoot camera takes the world's most beautiful pictures.

podcasting

precision handling

Remote-powered mini SUV: Your kid's first car

Robocop (movie)

Satellite photography reveals…

self-cleaning home

Solar-powered cars use one-fourth of the gasoline.*

Star Trek: The Next Generation (TV show)

Stay ahead of the curve.

streaming video

string theory

surround-sound technology

Techno pop historian, _____,

10…9…8…7…6…shuttle countdown begins

Text messaging is faster than an email. You get a reply almost instantly.

The Big Bang Theory

The Big Bento Box of Unuseless Japanese Inventions (book by Kenji Kawakami)

the early adopters

the enterprise

The first kid on the block to have…

the first wave

the flying car

the new millennium

The secret camera helps you keep an eye on your kids throughout the day.

the world's smallest speakers

time capsule

turnkey solutions

virtual reality

Wanted: Cyberspace Engineer

What if your VCR could program itself?

Will your cell phone let you roam around the world?

Wired (magazine)

wireless speakers

You'll enjoy your season tickets more when you can check out the instant replays on your mini TV.

Your grandchildren send instant messages to their friends nonstop. Sign up now. And you'll actually get through to your grandkids, instead of always waiting for them to get off line.

You're never out of touch.

Zap the boring commercials at the press of a button.**

---

*For more "Rev It Up Car Words," check out the Appendix.

**But modern technology is scary to some people. Check out "The Seamy Underbelly of Modern Technology" in the Appendix.

LANGUAGE POLICE

The PC (politically correct) world that we live in today can be a minefield for well-intentioned copywriters, especially when it comes to choosing a simple pronoun! Do not automatically assume that your entire audience is male, even when you're selling high-tech gadgetry. Nothing will infuriate the female population more. (And Hell hath no fury like a Geekette scorned.) When in doubt, it's generally safer to use the female pronoun, as men aren't quite as likely to become so offended. (Please don't quote me on that! Also, guys: no letters. Thanks!)

4. You Will Achieve Peace of Mind

We all want to sleep better at night, instead of grinding our teeth with worry. And wouldn't it be great if some empathetic marketer could help us quiet our anxiety attacks instead of a sympathetic but expensive shrink? Peace of mind is a cherished commodity, and certain products and services naturally lend themselves to this kind of argument. Alleviate your prospect's fears by promising him enhanced security, and rest assured, your solicitations will be taken seriously. After all, peace of mind is the next best thing to mother love, and often, much more readily available.

After fifteen minutes in "sleep" mode, your laptop will shut off automatically.

child-safety caps

controls nicotine cravings for twelve hours in a row

crash-dummy tested

Creditors will no longer bang at your door.

Dedicated sherpas will guide you through our country's scenic moors.

environmentally safe

golden parachutes

"Here's another Checkpoint Charlie: if you see a windmill, you've gone too far."

"I would never do anything to hurt you," he hastened to reassure her.

idiot-proof

If an intruder ever enters your home, lights will flash, alarms will sound, and the police will call within five minutes.

If you have any questions or concerns, don't hesitate to call me.

If you start saving now, you'll have $2 million by the time you retire.

Imagine never having to worry about _____.

In certain corners of the world, wealthy Americans usually hire bodyguards.

In the top right-hand corner of your rearview mirror, a digital readout even tells
you whether you're driving east, west, north, or south.

insurance

- casualty insurance
- disaster insurance
- earthquake insurance
- fire insurance
- life insurance
- 9/11 insurance
- pet insurance

investment-grade stocks

It takes the guesswork out of _____.

Just press *82 to display your restricted phone number.

Just push play

Last year, ten million Americans discovered they were victims of identity theft.
Here's how to protect yourself.

living wills

Motion control sensors pick up subtle movements.

"Not on my watch."

office pension plans

Operators are standing by to assist you.

Our discreet money belt helps you blend into crowds. Certainly, your handbag
won't be a target any longer.

Our firm has very specific guidelines pertaining to retiring financial advisors.

Our lie detector is 99 percent accurate.

Our security staff never sleeps.

overdraft protection up to $10,000

"Park your money in a Swiss bank account," his divorce lawyer advised.

Passenger-side airbags deploy on contact.

pick-proof locks

_____ practically takes care of itself.

prenuptial agreement

References available upon request

safe and sound

safety first

school chaperone

security
- blanket
- checkpoint
- clearance

Since 9/11, security has been beefed up in airports from La Guardia to LAX.

social security

Take it easy.

tax shelter*

That's a no-brainer.**

The Cayman Islands are a tax haven.

The Road to Wealth: Everything You Need to Know in Good and Bad Times (book
        by Suze Orman)

The world's most secure seatbelt

There's nothing more to do.

There's safety in numbers.

user-friendly***

Want to prevent a copycat attack? Sic 'em with bomb-sniffing dogs!

We're on call twenty-four hours a day.

When in Rome, do as the Romans do.

With our sleeping pills, you won't have that groggy, hungover feeling the morning after.

You buy life insurance for the living.

You can protect your kids from growing up too fast.

You can't keep your kids out of trouble forever. But you can give them cell phones so they can call you for help.

You will never have to ask yourself, "What if?"

You'll never miss another call.

Your kids will improve their SAT scores by at least thirty points.

You're always in control.

You're always protected.

*See "For Richer or Richer," Section IV, 2.

**For more "Quick Words," check out the Appendix.

***See "You Will Be Modern and in Vogue," Section IV, 3.

> ## Word Jumble
> When is a foreign language not a foreign language? When it's written in English.
> If copy sounds like it was transliterated or written in code, it's often because the person writing it doesn't know her features from her benefits. Not to be anal, but a *feature* is some fact about the product that's listed in its specs. The *benefit* of that feature is subjective. Example: a computer chip that lets parents prevent their kids from visiting certain Internet sites is a feature. Claiming that this chip will prevent your kids from growing up too fast is one possible benefit (or drawback if you can't wait for your kids to leave the house!).

5. Sex Appeal

Sex sells. So feel free to stimulate your consumer with titillating words. But also recognize that the Internet has made sex so available that, these days, you may be better off dialing up the romance in your copy. Romancing the words is a lot more gratifying than romancing a stone (plus it's generally more palatable to clients). Let the personality of your product be your shepherd. (No Freudian jokes about staffs, please! Or cigars.) Whether you decide to make your copy subtly flirtatious or positively steamy, here's a list of phrases to get you in the mood.

A Streetcar Named Desire (play by Tennessee Williams)

A touch of lusty Italian Country vinegar spices up simple spinach salad.

All chocolates make you feel like you're in love. Ours also inspire lust

Backless gown exposes the nape and shoulders

Boy meets girl, boy loses girl, boy marries girl

come hither looks

Come visit exotic _____.

evocative

eye candy

Escape for a romantic tryst.

Experience the rapture of_____.

Far away, a songbird calls out to her mate.

hard bodies

He planted a small kiss just under her chin.

Her hair fell in soft waves around her face.

Imagine the two of you swaying to the beat of our beautiful island music.

In the cool shadows, he took her into his arms.

It has a mystical presence.

Kiss Me Kate (musical by Cole Porter)

One little pill frees you to be more spontaneous.

Our beautifully cut jeans flatter all body types.

Our sensuous cashmere line...

Our silk sheets conform to every curve.

pillow talk

salsa rhythms

She floated into the room like a scarf.

She had fantasized about this moment for months.

_____, she said, fetchingly.

She was so attracted to him that she had difficulty meeting his eyes.

She will enthrall you.

sensual textures

soft and silky tresses

Sparks flew.

Spike heels from _____. Make him drool like the dog he is

spring fever

Start a fire.

Steal an intimate moment together.

strangers in the night

Surrender to the spell of...

"Take me," she instructed.

The call of the siren was difficult to ignore.

The silk camisole skimmed her lithe figure.

The tension loomed between them like a third presence in the room.

There's an iridescent sheen on the water.

They carried on a torrid love affair for years.

They tangoed until dawn.

Think of it as an aphrodisiac.

Waves lap the shore.

What Women Want (movie)

Your hands will look younger, more touchable.

Word Up
Figure out fresh ways to convey that a product has sex appeal. Hint: Saying "it has sex appeal" isn't all that appealing, or sexy, or even... (I apologize for using an ellipsis there...and there...all of this talk about sex has gotten me completely distracted!)

Closing Arguments Exercise: Real Estate Lust

Write an ad to sell your apartment.

The company where you work has given you the dream opportunity of a lifetime—the chance to move to Bermuda to help open up a new office overlooking the pink beach. There's only one catch—right now, you live in an unspectacular studio apartment that you need to sell in a hurry. Your apartment has no view, no closet space, no air, no light, no fireplace, and while we're being honest, no real kitchen. Think about how to position its benefits. Will your prospect be better off financially (because your apartment is so cheap)? Do you live in a doorman building which could at least give your buyer some peace of mind? For the purpose of this exercise, strenuously avoid real estate clichés such as "prewar gem" and "cozy." Think outside the six-hundred-square-foot matchbox. After all, at one point you chose to live there, didn't you?

Closing Arguments Exercise Cheat Sheet: 5 Phrases to Experiment With

1. Walk to work. Think of all the money you'll save on taxis.
2. You'll never have to worry about living with the roommate from Hell.
3. The most private spot in the city
4. Your first real apartment
5. It's small, but it's better than paying rent to your parents.

And 1 Phrase to Avoid No Matter What:

Manhattan luxury! To your own product, be truthful. It's not only the right thing to do; it's eminently practical—especially since your prospects are going to have to see the place eventually.

Section V:
Choose Your Words Wisely

William Shakespeare was a bard and a scholar. But he was seriously wrong about something. A rose is not a rose by any other name. And neither is a petunia. Word selection is key. English is a language that is richly endowed, which can make the task of finding the right word difficult. Your choice of words will determine your tone and also whether your prospect will respond to your message. What's in a word? Only everything. There are fourteen groups of words to choose from.

1. Words That Interviewers Love
2. Promises, Promises
3. Words for the Upscale Market
4. Today's Words vs. Yesteryear's Words
5. Festive Words
6. Euphemisms
7. Words That Sound Like What They Mean
8. Casual vs. Formal Language

9. Flowery Language
10. Rhymes
11. Numbers, Weights, and Measurements
12. Latin Words, a.k.a. One Good Reason Not to Go Back to Your Roots
13. English as a Second Language
14. Words That Get You in the Mood (Not *That* Mood)

Find the ideal word to describe what you mean, and you can call yourself the Shakespeare of copywriters.

1. Words That Interviewers Love

It's called "chronic résumé fatigue." And it can be brought on by staring at hundreds of different type fonts containing too much "so what" content. The eyes of your potential employer glaze over, and almost by habit, the résumé that you spent so much time crafting gets put into some strange file, never to be looked at again. How can you prevent an interviewer from transforming into a character from *The Day of the Living Dead*? Cite your claims to fame without adornment. Do your homework and position your skills to match the job requirements. Put on your hiring manager hat (blue is always becoming) and craft the résumé that influences interviewers and wins jobs.

achievements	cum laude	featured in
awards	detail-oriented	finalist
best read	experience	fostered excellent working
citations	expertise	relationships
claims to fame	fact-checking	hard worker
coached	fast	high energy
credentials	fastidious	honor student

honoree

improved

industrious

innovative

leader

licensed

magna cum laude

manager

maven

organized

outgoing

outperformed

people skills

prize-winning

professional

published

Quark literate

quick learner

quick study

recognized

research skills

results

right-hand man
(or woman)

sales tripled

scholastic achievements

sold

specialist

taught

team player

turned around a limping
department

2. Promises, Promises

How did you feel the last time a politician promised that he would cut taxes, managed to get elected, and failed to follow through? (What, like that ever happened?) It's far better to under-promise and keep expectations low, and then turn around and impress prospects by over-delivering. Think about the offers that turn you on, and work with your clients to give your customers the same thrill. Remember this always: you're not just a busy worker bee drone without a brain. You're a savvy marketing consultant! Okay, Ms. Consultant, what are the six most popular words in the English language? For the purpose of direct mail, they're "free," "you," and "cancel at any time."

absolutely fabulous fashion finds

At just $50, it gives new meaning to the term "summer fling."

Chic, simple, and best of all, free

Dutch treat. We'll split the cost of your first three months

Enclosed, please find your no-more-excuses Savings Voucher.

Every time you use the card, you get cash back.

Feel free to splurge at our $99-and-under sale.

Freedom's just another word for no more late charges

Health, wealth, and happiness: Get two free months if you sign up now

Keep the *Hamburger* CD at no extra charge.

Keep what you like and return the rest. We'll even pay the postage.

If you don't agree that it's exactly like a facelift in a bottle...

If you're just not into it, it's okay to cancel. We promise that it won't hurt our feelings.

If you're not completely satisfied with your membership after the first year, we'll happily refund your dues.

If you're not fully convinced,

Simply take a photograph of this ad with your camera phone and email it to us.

Take it all off. (80 percent of it, anyway)

The best things in life are free. (Well, almost)

The cheapest eats in SoFi (South of Fifth Avenue)

The single woman's guide to eating out solo

There's no obligation.

Try it for a month at our risk.

You'll be the first to receive notices about special contests and fabulous freebies.

You're free to cancel at any time.

Zero fees. (Yes, it may take some getting used to)

LANGUAGE POLICE

Isaac Newton's first law of physics states that an object in motion tends to stay in motion. That's why negative option marketing is sometimes called "marketing by inertia." Some clubs send books to members with the understanding that these customers will be *automatically* charged unless they return the items. People hate returning stuff; hence, some sales stick because people are lazy. But just because they're lazy doesn't mean that you can afford to be! Spell out the club policy. If an offer has strings, don't string your customer along, or he may become so strung out that he'll walk away forever.

3. Words for the Upscale Market

Wealthy people love to escape from their posh surroundings, even if they are only escaping to the privacy of their bathtubs. When writing to this market, use words that connote serenity, accommodating service, and the absence of masses of people. (However, if you tend to think, "Life is unfair," never take a job writing upscale solicitations because here the laws of capitalism definitely apply!) There is an inverse relationship between exclusivity and accessibility: the more exclusive the experience, the harder it will be for most people to enjoy it—either because it's exorbitantly expensive or located far away from their global villages.

A four-star chef will prepare a private meal for you and your loved one.
a hushed ambience
A stretch limousine will pick you up at the airport, drive you to Daniel, and wait
    for you while you nosh.
all of the accoutrements
amenities
box seats
by invitation only
cell-free zone
civilized
custom-tailored
designer
discreet
E
eighteen-karat
Enjoy the restorative powers of our citrus-scented bath salts.

exclusive

executive privileges

executive suite

first class

first discovered by the superaristocracy in Europe

four-diamond service

four-star service

French pedicures

French perfumes

genuine leather upholstery

Give yourself a psychological tune-up. Spend a few hours pampering yourself at
our spa.

gourmet

gracious and spacious

haute couture

Have dinner at the captain's table.

Imagine being personally serenaded by crooner _____.

in-room massages ease sore muscles

Leaning back on your private yacht as the sun sets over the Peconic Bay...

Listen to live jazz in our discreet lounge while sipping a cosmopolitan.

luxe

luxurious

Name a constellation for the one you love.

no preset spending limit

one-of-a-kind

One of our stylists will be happy to hand-dye your fur to match your hair color.

Our tailors are gifted at reconfiguring these elegant suits to flatter real curves.

Perched on the most exclusive golf course in the States, your cabin is equipped
with all of the civilized amenities that you'd expect.

personal

- fashion stylist
- secretary
- shopper
- trainer

posh

Practiced for just a few minutes each day, the ancient Eastern practice of yoga
can help you control breathing, meditate, and escape from the bustle of city
life.

premiere

private horseback riding lessons

red carpet

refined

retreat

sample sale for our best customers

serene

Spend an afternoon getting to know the real you. Step into our luxurious isolation tank

the billionaires' club

The Hamptons nobody knows. Spend a day parasailing through the North Fork

The loudest sound that you'll hear are the cries of hawks circling high overhead.

There are no groups of tourists jostling you.

to critical acclaim

To get accepted, you will need five recommendations from members.

unwind at our poet's retreat

upscale

urbane

valet parking

Visitors are politely dissuaded.

We attend to your every whim.

We'll deliver the libretto to you before you attend the opera that evening.

whisks you a million miles away from reality

You have been specially selected...

You'll feel as if you're on your own private island.

You'll find your inner voice at our writer's retreat, located in the beautiful Berkshires.

your chauffeur

your own private valet

Your privacy is assured.

Word Up

Do you need to attract a well-heeled clientele? Invite them to join the club. Call the select club by the name of a color, and you'll have the rich and near-rich banging at the proverbial door to get in. (Want to choose different hues? To find every color in the rainbow and then some, see the list of colors in the appendix.)

Black Label	Red Label	Green Card	Platinum Card
Purple Label	Blue Card	Gold Card	Silver Card

4. Today's Words vs. Yesteryear's Words

Copywriting is a constantly evolving art form. Phrases go in and out of style faster than hippie-chick hairstyles. (What? They're not in anymore?) Even core concepts can't withstand the test of time forever. So keep your finger on the pulse of language. Check out magazines; watch late night talk shows; and listen to radio news to find out what's more chill than cool right now. One caveat: keep your business writings in your own voice, and don't try to mimic your rave, downtown cousin's. Nothing ages a piece of copy faster than a writer trying to sound younger or more citified than she really is. Talk about urban angst!

Today's Words	Yesteryear's Words
"aha!" moment	epiphany
bipolar	manic depressive
black holes	little black dresses
blogosphere	biosphere
booty call*	little something on the side
brand	logo
Brazilian	bikini wax
carb out	binge
cell	going mobile
cyber nets	fishnets
dating your husband	dating your boyfriend
detox	rehab
drama queen	Jewish American Princess
"Email me."	"My people will call your people."

Emotional Intelligence	I.Q.
(book by Daniel Goleman)	
extensions	Jersey Girl hair
face time	"Let's get together."
Follow your gut.	E.S.P.
geeks	nerds
global warming	Rainforest deforestation
He's Just Not That into You	commitmentphobe
(book by Greg Behrendt and Liz Tuccillo)	
hooking up	dating
hot	cool
"I need some ME time."	"Let's spend some quality time
	together."
"I'm having difficulty processing that."**	"I can't deal with it."
"I'm outtie."***	"Let's make this place history."
Indulge your inner goddess.	Find your inner child.
interface	connect
Internet dating	Met at a fern bar.
laptop	word processor
"Let's take a time out."	"We need to talk."
life coaching	psychoanalysis
lip sync	synchronicity
martini	tequila sunrise
mini	maxi
meds	Rx

out-of-box experience	out-of-body experience
PMSed out****	"It's that time of the month."
pouty lips	killer smile
real estate bubble	dotcom bubble
text message	telegram
The Art of Seduction (book by Robert Greene)	*The Art of War* (book by Sun Tzu)
"The Gates" (art installation by Christo and Jeanne-Claude)	The Doors (band)
The O.C. (TV show)	*Beverly Hills, 90210* (TV show)
to Google	to ogle
trend spotting	*Trainspotting* (movie)
'tude	in your face
ultra-rich	well-to-do
unghosted autobiography	ghostwritten
"Want to meet for a tall, skim, double shot of espresso?"	"Let's grab a cup of Joe."

---

*See "Euphemisms" for *lust,* Section V, 6.

**Check out "The Seamy Underbelly of Modern Technology" in the Appendix.

***See "Valley Girlisms," Section V, 13.

****See "Words That Get You in the Mood (Not *That* Mood)," Section V, 14.

WORD JUMBLE

Over time, the meanings of words change ever so subtly, and what was once an insult can suddenly metamorphasize into a compliment! The word "geek" is no longer a synonym for "nerd," although both geeks and nerds tested well in high school and may have had a fondness for the Math Club. Today, geeks are wealthy, technologically savvy, and poised to continue to thrive in the new economy. They're the new Big Men On Campus, now that the "campus" happens to be real life.

5. Festive Words

Everyone loves a good party. It's an excuse to escape from the humdrum rhythm of our lives. And unlike junior high school, we don't have to be mega popular to score an invitation. Fact: only one person in a thousand was ever voted Prom Queen. The rest of us will feel like royalty just to be asked to your event! Whether you're writing to the nerds who blossomed into billionaires or those artistic types who are now writing books about writing, make your event sound like both conversation and cocktails will flow.

anniversary

- first-
- golden-
- silver-

bacchanal

birthday bash

- Lordy, 40!
- sweet 16

black tie

bubbly

celebrate

Christmas is in the air.

Cinco de Mayo (May 5th)

Come let others have a chance to get to know you.

Come schmooze and be schmoozed.

Create your own mojito. Twenty-four custom-blended flavors

confetti

dance marathon

Dance under the moon.

debauchery

den of iniquity

do-si-do

Dress up as your favorite celebrity.

entertaining

escapades

extravaganza

festive attire (Wear a tux, if you're feeling really festive.)

fete*

frolic

gaming

girls gone wild

girls' night out

Hawaiian shirts are mandatory.

hedonism

high-octane entertaining**

honeymoon

hors d'oeuvres at 7 p.m. in the Billiards Room

"I'm game."

island hopping

jamboree

joyous

lively

March madness

masquerade ball

Master the Brazilian samba.

maypole

meet and greet

Merry Christmas

mistletoe

Oktoberfest

orgy

paint the town red

party

party animal

playful

playpen

pop a cork

put on your dancing shoes

recreational

revelry

romp

second honeymoon

share a drink or a laugh

shop around the clock

shop till you drop

spring fever

spring fling

square dance

summer vacation

Swing bands will take you back.

theme parties

toast the New Year

velvet ropes

white tie

*See "French Words That You Hear Bandied About," Section V, 13.

**For more "Fun, Fun, Fun Words," check out the Appendix.

Watch Your Language

Some words that convey a party atmosphere also carry a double meaning that can be quite nega-tive. That's because at a certain point in the evening, a party often becomes too crowded, striking fear in the hearts of all but the most extroverted. Think carefully before describing anything as a "circus," "pleasure dome," "zoo," or "frat house." (Hey, I liked Sigma Chi parties, too, but c'mon!)

6. Euphemisms

Euphemisms are words and phrases that allude to your meaning without ever quite stating it. While you always want to be crystal clear, in certain special situations, you may need to use euphemisms. (Wait! Is that some sort of paradox? Yes, but riddle me this: if a client asks you to use euphemisms, what choice do you really have?) Clients know their customers, and the plain fact is, a lot of customers vastly prefer language that has been watered down. Know your audience! Carefully weigh the cost of "muddy copy" against the potential drawback of alienating a huge chunk of your target market. If you decide that euphemisms are needed, don't fret. Everyone on the planet will still know what you mean.

Euphemisms for "forgetful:"
ditzy
having a senior moment
loopy
spacing out (or "spaced")

Euphemisms for "homosexual:"
a lesbian, not the lipstick kind
alternative lifestyle
Are you sure he's into women?
"bears" (gay men who are proud of
    being hirsute)
effeminate
gaydar alert
gay vague ("He could be gay. He could
    be straight. I don't know... my gaydar
    is off.")
goes that way
He carries a handbag, but he's not
    European.
He has issues with women.
her beard
He's been outed.
He's into boys.
metrosexual (depends on the context)
on the D.L. (D.L. stands for "down
    low," as in secret.)
out of the closet
plays for the other team

same sex partner

still in the closet

swings that way (or "swings both ways")

switch hitter

They're like an old married couple.

Euphemisms for "love:"

He just "gets" me.

He swept me off my feet.

he's my friend/lover/partner

He's my main squeeze.

I adore you.

She's my better half.

soul mate

The chemistry's there.

The One

the real thing

They're attached at the hip.

They're totally inseparable.

We can't live without each other.

We're compatible.

We're exclusive.

When I first saw him, I just "knew."

Euphemisms for "lust:"

Blue binning (recycling, a.k.a. re-dating an ex)

can't keep his hands to himself

carnal pleasure

did the dirty

first, second, third, fourth base

for a good time, call...

gets me hot and bothered

gets me wet

gets my mojo working

getting it on

going around the bases

He's an animal.

He's just a good friend.

hooking up

I fantasize about him nonstop.

I had a dream about you.

in the mood

"key" parties

Let's get it on.

Let's get naked.

made his pupils dilate

makes me cream my jeans

need a cold shower

no-strings sex

randy

rendezvous

Sex with him is a workout.

"Three times a night... Why? How often do you guys...?"

turns me into jelly

"We went at it like..."

"We're 'friends plus.'"

When I get that feeling

Euphemisms for "overweight:"

a big girl

chubby

curvy

"Do I look fat?"

Fat Actress (TV show)

filled out

extra padding

He's got a gut.

Her skirts look a little tight.

hippy

love handles

pleasantly plump

plus-sized

put on a little

She could stand to lose ten pounds.

She doesn't exactly get lost in a crowd.

She has quite a presence.

She knows how to fill a room.

She's got three chins.

solid

still has some "baby fat"

super-sized

The Forgotten Woman (store)

the freshman fifteen

voluptuous

Word Up

The phrase "sensitive skin" covers every skin condition from acne to scales to rosacea to psoriasis—with an economy of words.

Euphemisms for "adverse skin conditions:"

sensitive skin

7. Words That Sound Like What They Mean

It's called "onomatopoeia," which certainly doesn't sound like what it means! Words that sound like what they mean add rhythm and tone to your copy. But, like fine French perfume, a little onomatopoeia goes a long way. Dab just a little, rather than dousing your copy with it, and your business writing will maintain an aura of sophisticated fun. Exclamation points add volume, particularly when you're playing with these evocative words. You may want to dial down the volume and let the words create their own natural buzz.

bang	hum	sneeze
break	hush	splash
buzz	kerplunk	splat
chirp	lash	squeak
choke	mumble	squeal
chug	murmur	shhh
crackle	meow	throttle
crash	pop	topsy-turvy
crunch	pow	tweet
erupt	purr	wham
fizz	ring	whiplash
gargle	rip	whipped
groan	roar	whirl
gurgle	screech	whisper
gush	sizzle	whistle
hiss	slurp	whoosh
honk	snap	

Word Up

Edgar Allen Poe's poem "The Bells" is a classic example of how onomatopoeia can be used to convey rhythm. Here is just a piece of his epic first stanza:

Keeping time, time, time,
In a sort of Runic rhyme,
To the tintinabulation that so musically wells
From the bells, bells, bells, bells,
Bells, bells, bells
From the jingling and the tinkling of the bells.

---

8. Casual vs. Formal Language

Now that we have casual Fridays at the workplace, surely the rules about business writing can be more relaxed, too. Not! Okay, but now that blogs are such a respectable marketing tool that even blue-chip companies are using them to reach out to consumers, we can all use more laid-back language to talk to these same folks, true? False, and by the way, a lot of folks hate being called "folks." Don't commit the sin of being too casual with your language if more formal language is expected, or vice versa. Would you call your best friend "Mr. Smith"? Would you address a distinguished Nobel laureate, "Hey, Joe"?

Casual Language	Formal Language
according to	pursuant to
Best,	Sincerely,
Big hug,	Love,
Dear John,	Dear Mr. Mueller,
Dear Mary,	Dear Mary Wilcox:
et cetera	_____(just complete the thought)
event	scenario

He walked the walk and talked the talk.	He was a Harvard MBA.
I'm delighted to let you know	I'm pleased to inform you
latest	state-of-the-art
Let's meet at twelve-ish.	Let's meet at noon.
m.o.	secret agenda or plan
Many thanks.	Thank you.
micro	small
number of eyeballs	number of people who watched the program
plugged in	connected
popspeak	clichéd phrases or slang from today's popular culture
psychobabble	psychologically inclined
therefore	ergo
things fizzled	terminated, divorced
two-faced	schizophrenic
two thumbs up	I think you'll agree that it's time well spent.
schedule	agenda
upwardly mobile	affluent
We're having some weather.	Tonight's forecast: severe rain storms.

{ **LANGUAGE POLICE**

Emotional intelligence is a combination of knowing what's appropriate for a piece of copy and also how far you can push the envelope. Be wary of bandying psychological terms such as "psychobabble" and "schizophrenic." You may mean them to convey a light tone, but there may be someone who receives your letter who won't be amused (and then you really will see Sybil's dark side). }

9. Flowery Language

Is there a place for language that brings us back to a bygone era? Formal, ornate language sounds odd to our ears, mainly because we don't hear it often. Blame it on the fact that there never seems to be enough time to take in a nineteenth-century classic (unless it's animated…sigh, don't get me started). However, in certain ritualized communications such as thank-you notes and condolence letters, flowery language adds a certain tone-appropriate flourish that will make readers appreciate your command of etiquette. Just don't ruin the impression by sending a thank-you email for a gift or a condolence email! As Marshall McLuhan said, the medium is the message. If you're using flowery language, your "medium" really needs to be a handwritten note on engraved stationery.

A Heartbreaking Work of Staggering Genius (book by Dave Eggers)

Best wishes,

"Dan's reputation precedes him. You are already familiar with the wonderful work that he has done for our temple."

"Do you take this woman to be your lawfully wedded wife, till death do you part?"

ensemble

Everyone who's anyone will be there.

Fellow countrymen, I implore you...

"Four years ago, when I entered these ivy-covered walls, it never occurred to me that..."Good morning, Mrs. Peters.

"How do you do?"

"How many people here today have ever lost a loved one? May I have a show of hands, please?"

I can't thank you enough for your lovely gold lamé finger bowls.

I know one little boy whose heart is set on...

"I pledge allegiance to the flag of the United States of America" (original Pledge of Allegiance by Francis Bellamy)

"I want to thank you all for coming here today. And now I know that you are eager for the festivities to start."

I was saddened to hear that your father had passed away. If there is anything that I might do to help ease the pain,

in the event that

"In Xanadu did Kubla Khan / A stately pleasure-dome decree..." ("Kubla Khan" by Samuel Taylor Coleridge)

"It gives me enormous pleasure to introduce..."

Joanna L. Knightsbridge, beloved wife, mother, daughter, and friend,

Kindly refrain from using your cell phones.

"Ladies and gentlemen,"

"Let me do the honors."

"Many happy returns."

"Mary, we will always be grateful for all the contributions you've made to our company..."

might (as a verb)

Mr. and Mrs. Geoffrey Strauss are pleased to announce the marriage of their daughter, Violet Ann Strauss, to

Mr. and Mrs. Steven Sommers joyfully announce the arrival of Samantha, December 20, 2007.

Once upon a time,

"Pardon me,"

red carpet premiere

_____ requests the honor of your presence

_____ requests the pleasure of your attendance

Respectfully yours,

Summa cum laude (with highest distinction)

"That would be no trouble at all, Mrs. Sullivan."

The Conroys accept your gracious invitation with pleasure.

"The defense rests."

The engagement of Ms. Mary C. Carter and Mr. Joshua L. Spalding has been broken by mutual consent.

The favor of a reply is requested.

the great and the near great

The McIntyre family gratefully acknowledges your kind gift.

To whom it may concern:

"We are gathered here today to honor a woman who has selflessly devoted herself to..."

We are writing today to seek nominations and applications from our entire college community for the position of president of the Alumni Association.

"We hold these truths to be self-evident, that all men are created equal..." (Declaration of Independence, Thomas Jefferson)

Will you grace us with your presence?

without prejudice (for legal matters)

your attendance is cordially requested

Yours truly,

WORD JUMBLE

When using the language of flattery, make sure that it's not so exclusive that it excludes your reader. Don't write: *Everyone who's anyone will be there. Can we also count on you to come join us?* (It sounds like everyone who's anyone is already there. And that there is a third category of invitees: total nobodies like your reader!)

10. Rhymes

As infants, our first sentence was "Mama." Our second sentence was, "Rock-a-bye baby, in the treetops." And, as we got older, rhymes continued to bring us back to that magical minute when we were masters of the universe in our cribbed domains. For this very reason, most copy should not rhyme (unless you're a poet, in which case, go right ahead). But occasionally, you might want to use words that rhyme for effect. If your words are end-rhymes, you might be able to get away with using them in a serious piece of copy. Sometimes, two words can even rhyme all the way through without resorting to phrases that are brutally cute.

accessorize	felicity
itemize	tenacity
organize	veracity
prioritize	
	CEO
adaptive	CFO
perceptive	echo
receptive	
	cheat
address	sheet
impress	
suppress	cinematic
transgress	emblematic
	erratic
aggravate*	ecstatic
irritate*	conviction
audacity	prediction

exotic

quixotic

hideous

insidious

I hope, you hope.

We all hope

for cantaloupe!

malleable

reliable

meander

pander

coriander

meditate

levitate

asphyxiate

morph

Bergdorf

nation

elation

syncopation

radio station

percolate

premeditate

perambulate

postulate

demonstrate

pliable

viable

stay

stray

eBay

surrender

pretender

thin

hatpin

chagrin

think

pink

white knight

sit tight

incite

outtasight!

widget

gadget

budget

wedding

vetting

---

*For other "Commonly Confused Words," check out the Appendix.

WATCH YOUR LANGUAGE

When it comes to rhymes, it turns out there's a gender gap! Rhymes of single, accented syllables ("brutally cute") are masculine, while rhymes that last for two syllables in which the first syllable is stressed ("reliance/science") are feminine. Okay, masculine rhymes on one side of the page, feminine rhymes on the other…

11. Numbers, Weights, and Measurements

Most of us grew up thinking of English and math as entirely separate disciplines. Just flash back to your SAT scores. (Do I have to? Yes, you have to!) What's the bottom line today? There is a lot more math encoded into the English language than ever before, and as we evolve into a 24/7 computer-driven, cell-phone-centric, and text-message friendly society, the number of math-based English words continues to grow exponentially. It's a numbers game. As a writer, you can choose to fight the trend if you will. Or you can embrace "the math of English" with the numerous lists of numbers-oriented phrases below.

One

Formula One

Give him an inch and he'll take a mile.

He scored in the top 1 percent of the nation.

numero uno

one hand washes the other

one-on-one communication

One plus one is two.

one, two, buckle my shoe

Once upon a time,

only child

solitaire

solitaire diamond

solitary confinement

World War I

Two

biannual

bicentennial

biceps

bicoastal

bifocals

bilateral

bimonthly column

binary system

binoculars

bipolar disorder

bisect

bisexual

clone

couples

couplets

Coupling (TV show)
double down
double trouble
duet
duo
He's the CEO's number two.
ice skating pairs
identical twins
It takes two to tango.
second helping
the dynamic duo
The Odd Couple (TV show)
Twin Towers
2+2=4
two-year colleges
twofer'
World War II

the tri-state area
The Triangle Trade
third base
third generation wealth
Three Dog Night (band)
three's a charm
Three's Company (TV show)
Three of Wands
threesome
triangle
trifecta
trilogy
trinity
triple axle
triple threat
triplets
tripod

Three

Pi (3.1415926)
Terminator 3 (movie)
The Bermuda Triangle
The Three Stooges (TV show)
The Three Tenors

Four

all fours
"Check out the girl at four o'clock."
four corners
"Four more years!"
four of a kind

four seasons

foursome

the four basic food groups (grains, vegetables, meat, dairy)

the four humors (earth, wind, fire, water)

the 411 (information)

Five

Dave Clark Five (band)

Fifth Business (book by Robertson Davies)

fifth wheel

five o'clock shadow

five-paragraph essay

Five Points (neighborhood)

five senses

high-five

"I take the Fifth."

Slaughterhouse-Five (book by Kurt Vonnegut)

the five and dime store

The Five O'Clock Club

Six

double sixes

"I'm at sixes and sevens."

Lover's leap (a roll of six and five in the game of backgammon)

PAGE SIX

Rocky VI (movie)

Route 66

sextuplets

6 Degrees of Separation (play by John Guare)

Six Feet Under (TV show)

triple six (a Devil's number, considered evil and extremely unlucky)

Seven

On the seventh day, He rested.

"One, two, three, four, five, six, seven. All good children go to heaven..." (nursery rhyme)

seven chakras (back of spine, womb, solar plexus, heart, throat, third eye, crown of head)

seven continents

seven days a week

seven deadly sins (envy, greed, lust, gluttony, pride, sloth, wrath)*

7-11

Seven Layer Cake

seven wonders of the world

Seventh Heaven (TV show)

the seven dwarves (Bashful, Dopey, Grumpy, Happy, Sleepy, Sneezy, and Doc)**

The Seven Habits of Highly Effective People (book by Stephen R. Covey)

The Seven Sisters (Barnard, Bryn Mawr, Mount Holyoke, Radcliffe, Smith, Vassar, Wellesley)

The seven-year itch

Eight

behind the eight ball

eight hours of sleep

Eight Is Enough (TV show)

Eight is the third number that stays the same when it's written upside down.

eight-legged insects

8 Mile (movie)

eight-track

Henry VIII (Henry VIII had six wives: Catherine of Aragon, Anne Boleyn, Jane Seymour, Anne of Cleves, Kathryn Howard, and Katherine Parr.)

If you place an eight on its side, it turns into infinity.

place the eight ball in the pocket

teaching K–8

V-8 engines

Nine

a 917 cell phone number

Baseball has nine players on each side.

Cats have nine lives.

cloud nine

nine-digit security code

nine-digit social security number

9/11

nine months of pregnancy

nine planets (Mercury, Venus, Earth, Mars, Jupiter, Saturn, Uranus, Neptune, Pluto)

9-to-5 mentality

the whole nine yards

Ten

a #10 envelope

Count to ten before getting angry.

decathlon

hang ten

She's a ten.

ten digits

Ten-four, good buddy.

The Big Ten (men's college basketball teams: Illinois, Michigan State, Wisconsin, Minnesota, Indiana, Ohio State, Iowa, Northwestern, Michigan, Purdue, Penn State. Yes, there are eleven teams in the Big Ten.)

the decimal system

The Ten Commandments

the zero's column

Twelve and Over

Agent 99

Around the World in Eighty Days (book by Jules Verne/movie)

baker's dozen (means thirteen)

centipede

do a 180

eight million New Yorkers

80 percent of the people make 20 percent of the money.

Eighty-seven, the national average for a woman's life expectancy today

50-50 chance

Fifty is the new forty.

Forbes 400

Fortune 500

Friday the thirteenth

Hindsight is 20/20.

Hits from the '70s, '80s, and '90s

Lower 48 (states)

Oldies station

Seventeen (magazine)

76,000 fans (capacity of Giant's Stadium)

60 Minutes (TV show)

69 (sexual position)

the 24/7 world we live in

thirtysomething (TV show)

301 Smart Answers to Tough Interview Questions (book by Vicky Oliver)

360 degrees (full circle)

twelve signs of the Zodiac (Aries, Taurus, Gemini, Cancer, Leo, Virgo, Libra, Scorpio, Sagittarius, Capricorn, Aquarius, Pisces)

twelve hundred square foot apartment

twelve-step program

twenty-nine and holding

20 percent of the people spend 80 percent of the money.

20/20 vision

2,000 MB storage

unlucky thirteen

Welcome to the twenty-first century.

Fractions

always sees the glass half full

Half and Half

"Half lit, someone loves you."

half-off sale

how the other half lives

"Let's go halvsies."

my better half

the top tenth of 1 percent

Words and Phrases That Convey Numbers (Without Citing Any Numbers)

a gaggle of geese

a school of fish

a woman of a certain age

an exultation of larks

"blackjack"

coming of age story

digital age

double-digit inflation

drinking age

exponentially

Generation X

He was in his prime.

in his infinite wisdom

"Let's split the difference."

mega

Mensa club***

middle age

multiple

multiplex

multiplied

nanoseconds

numerology

old enough

  • to be drafted

  • to be his mother

  • to have a learner's permit

  • to vote, but not to drink

paint by numbers

R rating

Senior Lit****

She could hear her biological clock
  ticking.

She was in the winter of her life.

shooting the moon

size matters

The Infinite Mind (radio program)

the long and the short of it

---

*Check out "The 7 Deadly Copywriting Sins" in the Appendix.

**See "Words That Get You in the Mood (Not *That* Mood)," Section V, 14.

***For more "Super Intelligent Words," check out the Appendix.

****Check out "Genres," in the Appendix.

Word Up

When a man asks a woman to get married, it's interesting that he often starts the union by giving her an engagement ring with a *solitaire* diamond. What are the 3 C's of writing flawless copy? 1) Clarity—Make it clear. 2) Color—Make it interesting. 3) Cut—edit ruthlessly.

12. Latin Words, a.k.a. One Good Reason Not to Go Back to Your Roots

Thirty-eight years before the year 1984, George Orwell wrote "Politics and the English Language." In this essay, Orwell warned against using streams of words with Latin or Greek roots, arguing that it made writers sound pretentious. Want to use them anyway? Do yourself a favor and make sure you know what they mean. There's nothing more annoying than a writer who misuses big, long words. That's not just pretentious, but arrogant and foolish. (I used up my daily ration of adjectives in that sentence. Mea culpa!) In this list, find some words that irked Orwell; cut the *extraneous* ones, and use the rest at your own discretion.

ameliorate	extraneous
clandestine	liquidate
deracinated	predict
expedite	subaqueous

Word Up
According to Webster's, the word "deracinated" means "to pluck up by roots." Who knew?

13. English as a Second Language

America is one giant melting pot and the language that we speak today is a rich mixture of words with roots from Old English, German, Anglo-Norman, Gaelic, Greek, Latin (sorry, Orwell!), French, Spanish, and Native American. The Industrial Revolution created a need for new words for ideas that had never existed before. Today, the Internet revolution is also responsible for spawning a slew of new words such as *byte, cyber,* and *microchip.* Perhaps because the Internet has made everyone more comfortable coexisting in a 24/7 "world community," foreign words are being imported into spoken English at the speed of sound.

Yiddish That's Made Its Way into Spoken English

chutzpah: ballsy

gelt: money

kibitz: to meddle

mazl-tov: congratulations

mentsch: a person with a good character

nosh: a light snack

"oh vey": "oh my goodness!"

schlemazel: unlucky person

shikse: non-Jewish female

shlemil: fool

shlep: to carry

shmates: rags, clothing ("the shmates industry")

shtik: routine

tsures: trouble

French Words That You Hear Bandied About*

a la carte: on the menu (meaning that customers pay for each item on the menu separately)

à la mode: with ice cream

avant-garde: on the cutting edge

bon bons: candy

"bon voyage": "have a great trip"

café au lait: coffee with a lot of milk (often served in a bowl)

carte blanche: unlimited authority

cherchez la femme: look for the woman

"comme ci, comme ça": "things are so-so"

coup de grace: a decisive act that brings about a drastic change

croissant: a flaky pastry in the shape of a crescent

demimonde: a class of women who are supported by wealthy lovers; a group whose respectability is dubious

demitasse: half a cup; a small cup of coffee used to serve Turkish coffee or espresso

duck l'orange: duck with orange sauce

Elle (magazine): she

esprit de corps: morale

extraordinaire: excellent

faux pas: mistake; a violation of an accepted (although unwritten) social rule

fait accompli: a done deal

ingénue: a naïve girl or young woman; an actress playing that role

laissez faire: leave it alone; don't get involved

mariage blanche: a sexless marriage

ménage a trios: a sexual encounter with three people

menagerie: a zoo

"Merci beaucoup!": "Thanks a lot!" (often said sarcastically)

nom de plume: pen name; an invented name under which an author writes

nouveau riche: newly rich; term to describe people who acquire wealth within one generation and then often go on to spend the money lavishly

objet d'art: an art object

pièce de résistance: the highlight

"plus ça change, plus c'est la meme chose": "the more things change, the more they remain the same"

prix fixe: a fixed price charged for a meal, often including several courses

rendezvous: a meeting

tête-à-tête: a one-on-one conversation

tour de force: a feat of strength

très: very

Vogue (magazine): fashion

"Voulez vous couches avec moi sur soir?": "Will you sleep with me tonight?"

*Also check out "More Words from Our Distinguished Wines and Spirits Collection," in the Appendix.

Valley Girlisms (to Be Avoided, Like, at All Costs)

"As if!"

Been there, done that.

copasetic

da da da

"Don't even think about it."

"Don't go there!"

dude

"Duh!"

"End of story!"

"Excuse me?"

He couldn't deal with it.

"He was, like, into, like…"

"Hello?"

frickin'

"Get outta here!"

gnarly

"Good looking? Oh puh-*leeze!*"

groovy wa

"I am so over him."

"I don't think so."

"I thought I was being reasonable, but whatever!"

"I'm outtie."

"Kiss, kiss."

"Let's have some gratitude attitude."

"Let's not go there."

"Like, just fill in the blanks."

"No way, José!"

"Oh, man!"

Ohmigod

rad

tubular

"What part of 'no' don't you understand?"

She just freaked out.

She quasi went ballistic.

sooo

ta-da!

to die for

totally!

"Yesss!"

"You go, girl!"

"you know,"

"You're killin' me!"

From the 'Hood

baby mama: the mother of one's child

bling: shiny, flashy jewelry

bodega: corner store

boo: boyfriend or girlfriend

booty: buttocks (normally female)

chill: to hang out, relax

da': the ("He's da' man.")

da bomb: appealing or popular

diss: to show disrespect for someone; to insult someone

"I'm down with that": "I agree"

jonesing: to have a strong desire or craving for something ("I'm jonesing for a hot date.")

mack daddy: someone who is gifted with the opposite sex

my bad: my mistake

phat: good; the acronym for Pretty Hot and Tempting

playa: someone who plays the field

posse: one's crowd

"'Sup?": "What's up?"

V-card: virginity—all virgins have a V-card until they give it up for sex ("Who cashed in her V-card?")

wack: crazy, screwed up

"What up?": "How are you doing?"

Business Slang

COB: close of business

EOW: end of week

He was kicked upstairs: Sometimes, this means "promoted." Sometimes, it simply means "he was kicked upstairs to a position where he could do no harm."

kissing up

let's knock some ideas around and see if they stick: brainstorm

pencil pushers: people who add no value to a project or company

play hardball

schmoozing: networking, particularly while one is wining and dining

sweeten the deal

the donut guy: someone who contributes little to meetings

the golden boy: the one whom the boss favors

the whipping boy: the one whom the boss blames, often unfairly

{
WORD JUMBLE
Do a mitsve (good deed) and don't use words like "shlemil" and "shlemazl" unless you can define the difference. You don't want people to start kvetshing (complaining) about your word usage! To be perfectly clear: a "shlemil" is one who always spills his soup. A "shlemazl" is the one on whom it always lands. Mazl-tov!
}

14. Words That Get You in the Mood (Not *That* Mood)

What's in a mood? A color, if you happen to be in a blue mood. A budding migraine if you're feeling anxious. Or a raging thunderstorm, if you're angry with someone. Moods are contagious. If you have enough willpower, you can even "will yourself" into a better mood. How do you capture a mood on paper? You can compare the feeling to something more tangible through a poetic metaphor, or you can strip away the verbiage, and, good or bad, simply identify the mood for what it is. (It all depends on what kind of a mood you're in.) Put on your virtual mood ring and start writing. And if you're too young to know what a mood ring is, be happy.

agita	cranky
agitated	crazy
agony	delighted
all mixed up	deranged
alter ego	disturbed
angry	Dr. Jekyll and Mr. Hyde
antsy	edgy
anxiety attack	excited
anxious	fearless
argumentative	feel incredibly guilty
beside herself	focused
beyond exhausted	foul
bitterness	furious
Borderline Personality Disorder (BPD)	going through the motions
chillin'	"Great to see you too," she snickered.
chomping at the bit	grief-stricken
combustible	hair trigger
confused	hungover

in desperate need of some shut eye

in the zone

indifferent

introverted

irate

irked

irritated

jumping up and down

kicking back

manic

nervous laughter

on auto pilot

on cruise control

on edge

out of his mind with grief

pacing back and forth

peeved

pissed off

playing head games

PMSed-out

pooped

pulling out his hair

recharge your batteries

saddened

schadenfreude (taking delight in other people's misery)

serene

silly

stressed out

stressed to the max

stretched too thin

strung out

Sybil

tapping his foot

ticked off

venomous

wacked

wigging out

zoned out

zonked

{ ## LANGUAGE POLICE

If you were to rank types of words in terms of their strength (what, doesn't everyone do this?), adjectives would be the weakest, with adverbs a close second. Often there's nothing inherently wrong with the adverb itself. The problem is that the writer has chosen a modifier that doesn't add anything new to the reader's understanding of the situation. *"Cut!" the director screamed, tapping her fingers on the camera nervously.* (Did you really need to read the word "nervously" to understand what was happening? Excellent.) }

Choose Your Words Wisely Exercise: Girls Gone Wild (and Boys)

Write an invitation to a party that you want to throw.

Pretend it's a Hawaiian-themed bash in the dead of winter. What kind of music will there be? What would you like the guests to wear? Will the drinks be shaken, stirred, or blended? Will each guest be allowed to bring someone with him? Do you want presents? Put some joy into your invitation: use festive words. Take ten minutes and write out your invitation now. Once you love it, send it out to people. There's no time like the present to practice your writing and drinking skills (hopefully in that order!).

Choose Your Words Wisely Cheat Sheet: 5 Phrases to Experiment With

1. It's ten degrees outside. Snow is hugging the ground. It's time for a luau.
2. Mandatory dress code: leis, grass skirts, and Hawaiian shirts.
3. Win a pineapple cooler in the hula contest.
4. A live DJ will spin authentic island music.
5. Limbo on down to your local mailbox and RSVP now.

And 1 Phrase to Avoid, No Matter What:

B.Y.O.B. (If you're going to all the effort of throwing a theme party, why destroy the ambience with lousy donated Pinot Grigio?)

chiseled crotchety ecstatic conscientious genuine dour gripping magnetic nagging erratic spi
ky tenacity congenial titillating risque haughty enduring svelte poignant eccentric rich achieve a
llenge chop clarify commit craft create dramatize enhance erase finagle find finesse generate in
rrogate interrupt jump lead motivate nip organize oversee pepper pinch plan raise rally rouse
ke strategize surpass trump tweeze unveil win zoom striking appalling deadly manic inspired bleak
d disastrous exhilarating captivating outstanding wry chiseled crotchety ecstatic conscientious
 dour gripping magnetic nagging erratic spiritual cocky tenacity congenial titillating risque hau
uring svelte poignant eccentric rich achieve aspire challenge chop clarify commit craft create dr
enhance erase finagle find finesse generate inspire interrogate interrupt jump lead motivate nip o
oversee pepper pinch plan raise rally rouse save shake strategize surpass trump tweeze unvei
n striking appalling deadly manic inspired bleak rigid jaded disastrous exhilarating captivating
ding wry chiseled crotchety ecstatic conscientious genuine dour gripping magnetic nagging e
tual cocky tenacity congenial titillating risque haughty enduring svelte poignant eccentric rich ac
re challenge chop clarify commit craft create dramatize enhance erase finagle find finesse gen
ire interrogate interrupt jump lead motivate nip organize oversee pepper pinch plan raise rally r
 shake strategize surpass trump tweeze unveil win zoom striking appalling deadly manic inspired
 jaded disastrous exhilarating captivating outstanding wry chiseled crotchety ecstatic conscien
uine dour gripping magnetic nagging erratic spiritual cocky tenacity congenial titillating risque hau
uring svelte poignant eccentric rich achieve aspire challenge chop clarify commit craft create dr
enhance erase finagle find finesse generate inspire interrogate interrupt jump lead motivate nip or
oversee pepper pinch plan raise rally rouse save shake strategize surpass trump tweeze unvei
n striking appalling deadly manic inspired bleak rigid jaded disastrous exhilarating captivating
ding wry chiseled crotchety ecstatic conscientious genuine dour gripping magnetic nagging er
tual cocky tenacity congenial titillating risque haughty enduring svelte poignant eccentric rich ach
re challenge chop clarify commit craft create dramatize enhance erase finagle find finesse gene
re interrogate interrupt jump lead motivate nip organize oversee pepper pinch plan raise rally r
 shake nip striking appalling deadly manic inspired bleak rigid jaded disastrous exhilarating capt
outstanding wry chiseled crotchety ecstatic conscientious genuine dour gripping magnetic nag
ic spiritual cocky tenacity congenial titillating risque haughty enduring svelte poignant eccentric
eve aspire challenge chop clarify commit craft create dramatize enhance erase finagle find fin
erate inspire interrogate interrupt jump lead motivate nip organize oversee pepper pinch plan raise
e save shake strategize surpass trump tweeze unveil win zoom striking appalling deadly manic insp
k rigid jaded disastrous exhilarating captivating outstanding wry chiseled crotchety ecstatic cons

Section VI:
Product Attributes

The product is king (or queen, if you're a feminist). You must keep your copy focused on the product or service that you are selling, even if the product happens to be YOU. Don't go off on tangents, even if they're really interesting. This copywriting sin is called "borrowed interest," but it should be called "loses interest." Remember that your main task is to persuade, not to show off how creative you are. Don't obscure your product's attributes, or there will be little reason for you to be writing your solicitation in the first place.

There are five types of product attributes.

1. It's Healthy
2. It's Enduring
3. Look, Marge, How Convenient!
4. It's So Refreshing (or Relaxing)
5. It Makes a Statement

Always remember that your product is hero. Or heroine. Or a fluffy apricot poodle, if you're into dogs.

1. It's Healthy

The aging baby boomers were the first group of Americans who stubbornly refused to age. Because the boomers were very influential (and looked so damned good), every generation that followed them adopted the same Peter Pan credo. (Imitation *is* the sincerest form of flattery.) Today, everyone over a certain age looks and acts at least ten years younger than they really are, and fifty has become the new forty. But while an old adage claims that "looks are only skin deep," the new fixation with health and fitness runs far deeper, filtering down into thousands of food, beauty, and pharmaceutical product claims. Here's a healthy heaping of words that can help keep our collective metabolism up, our blood pressure down, and all of us looking forever young.

aerobic

ageless
- age-defying*
- age-proof
- age-resistant

all natural

alpha hydroxy

anaerobic

antioxidants

antiseptic

beta hydroxy

clean

contains
- aloe vera
- emollients
- Vitamin C

- Vitamin E

distortion-free lenses

Doctors use it on their own kids.

erases fine lines and wrinkles

farm fresh

fights
- acne (teenage)
- adult acne
- age spots and wrinkles
- creases
- gravity
- gray
- the visible signs of aging

filters out harmful rays

firms

germicidal protection

glowing

heart

- healthy
- smart

homegrown

homemade

Hospitals use it.

Inspected by #289

lifts sagging skin (and your spirits)

light

look only as old as you feel inside

made the old-fashioned way

mineral supplements for eyes (contains Lutein)

99 percent pure

no

- additives
- animals were tested
- carbs
- clumps
- peroxide
- preservatives

non-allergenic

nothing artificial

oil-free

100 percent of the daily minimum requirement

organic

perfume-free

plumps up your lips naturally

polarized lens

pore

- minimizing
- refining

protects against UVB rays

recommended by dentists

rehydrate your skin

SPF 45 (Sun Protection Factor)

safe sex

smile lines and crows feet vanish

solar-powered

speeds metabolism

spotless

spring water

sugar and starch-free**

sunless tanning

tightens

tones

toxin-free

untouched

*For more "Isn't She Lovely? Beauty Words," check out the Appendix.

**For more "Words to Diet for," check out the Appendix.

Word Up

In the real world, art and science rarely mingle. But in the world of advertising, art and science are totally inseparable. Flip through any glossy fashion magazine. Notice how many beauty ads make some kind of a scientific claim, be it a polymer that lengthens lashes by 50 percent, a diet pill that's been "scientifically proven" to nix cravings, or a lab-tested conditioner that restores locks to their original luster. There's an art to looking young and gorgeous: it's called science.

---

2. It's Enduring

Fashion is fickle, but longevity endures. One classic marketing technique is to describe your product as a classic (which can help customers leap over the hump of a steep price tag in their classic Keds sneakers). In a post-9/11 world where we can no longer count on anything to last forever, at least we can believe that some of our products and services will make good long-term investments! It may not sound frivolous or flirty or particularly fun, but it's solid. And who can argue with solid? Pretend that you're a financial planner if you have to. And position your product as the fashion/automotive/beauty equivalent of a risk-free mutual fund.

bedrock
built to a higher standard
built to last
classic rock*
faith in a higher power
"forever and ever, Amen"
gold standard

handcrafted to resist the wear and tear of everyday living

Here today, here tomorrow.

heredity

"He's 'executive material.'"

"He's 'good people.'"

He's her anchor.

If only everything you owned were as reliable.

"I'm there for you."

In a disposable world, it's made to last

in perpetuity

indelible impression

integrity

It may well outlast your spouse

It's a modern heirloom.

It's grilled slowly to seal in the flavor.

It's in it for the long haul.

It's made the old-fashioned way.

It's part of the literary canon.

lasts a lifetime

like a rock

longevity

oak tree

old money

Our computer system is scalable. As your company grows, it will grow right along with you.

pass on the torch

pillar

Please join us for our traditional Christmas eggnog.

put down roots in the community

solid as a rock

strong

surefire

ten-year warranty

tested by our engineers

The apple doesn't fall far from the tree.

The One**

the Rolls Royce of _____

time capsule

Time is on your side.

timeless classic

unshakable belief

unwavering

You can throw it, drop it, or stomp on it. It won't break.

"You're my rock."

*Check out "Genres" in the Appendix.

**See "Euphemisms" for *love,* Section V, 6.

***If you ever *have* considered a career in accounting, check out "How to Unblock Writer's Block (One Writer's Opinion)" in the Appendix.

{ **WATCH YOUR LANGUAGE**
Take care not to make your product sound like it's so solid that it's positively staid. As advertising legend David Ogilvy once said, "You can't bore a customer into a sale." (And even if you could, you shouldn't want to. If you can't take pride in the ads, brochures, and letters that you write, you shouldn't become a copywriter. There are far easier ways to make a living. Have you ever considered a career in accounting?)*** }

3. Look, Marge, How Convenient!

Stress is becoming a national obsession. With the advent of the Internet, email, cell phones, beepers, pagers, and the Blackberry, it's now possible to reach anyone at any hour of the day. Everyone feels overwhelmed, and the "burn out" factor is high. (Just ask any mom with two or more young kids how she feels on any given Wednesday at 7 a.m.) Considering the collective stress that we all face, sometimes simply claiming that a product is convenient is enough to sell it. Just don't mumble your message, or no one will hear it above the roar and clatter of kids rushing off to school and cell phones jangling in the background. Do you believe in love at first sight? Simply show a customer how your product was designed to make her life more organized, less mentally draining, and less frantic.

all the modern classics on audiotape
Attractive cell holster coordinates with any belt style.
Babysitter available on all national holidays
City storage. Out of sight, out of mind
cruise control
gourmet meals, microwavable in minutes
How to Pack Light on Your Next Business Trip
It does more.

- Digital display even tells you the name of the band and the song.
- It contains an alphabet soup's worth of vitamins.
- Protects against UVA, UVB, and jellyfish stings.

It does the work for you.

- It never forgets where you parked your car, even if you do.
- One pill, once a day, and your daily requirements are covered.

It fits your "on the go" lifestyle.

- disposable (anything)
- laptop
- modular furniture

It works its magic while you do something else.

- Renews skin while you sleep.
- Whitens teeth overnight.

It's always there when you need it.

It's barely there.

- compact
- cordless
- fits in a purse
- invisible
- mini
- virtual
- wireless

mistake-proof

one size fits all

one-stop shopping

Operators are standing by, twenty-four hours a day.

Pay for one pet shrink. Get a dog walker, plant person, and driver, absolutely free

Perhaps we can arrange a mutually convenient time to meet.

self-cleaning

Tell us the top ten things you're looking for in a mate, and we'll find your perfect match.

There's no downtime.

presto, change-o

This special water refreshes and revives while it sates your craving for nicotine.

There's no learning curve.

Top Five Beauty Items You'd Bring to a Desert Island

We'll be happy to talk you through the installation process.

We're here to serve you.

You are receiving this email because you requested it. If you would like to be taken off our mailing list, simply hit the link below.

your

- housecleaning genie
- personal assistant
- pocket assistant
- slave for a day

Word Up

Timing is everything. If your selling ideas are on trend, they will turn on masses of people. And if your ideas are off trend, you can shout them from the rooftops and no one will pay any attention. So if humanly possible, try to attach your product to a trend. Fact: Even though Americans are obsessed with health and fitness (see point one in this section), as a nation, we are more obese than ever. Is it any wonder that clothing which claims "one size fits all" continues to practically sell itself? Size matters. Apparently, so does the lack of it. (Now that that's settled, can you pass the bon bons, please?)

4. It's So Refreshing (or Relaxing)

The cure for too much tension (see point three in this section) is relaxation, hence the popularity of products that ease the burden of modern living by helping us to let go of our anxieties. These days, East meets West, as the five-thousand-year-old practice of yoga, the four-thousand-year-old tradition of feng shui, and the two-thousand-year-old practice of acupuncture are all hot right now in the U.S. Expect to read promises that play off ancient Eastern ideas of "balance," "harmony," and "positive energy flow." You may want to even craft a couple yourself. Just go easy on the ketchup. For some reason, feng shui never seems to work quite as well in a McMansion.

Aromatherapeutic candles soothe your mood. But be forewarned: one visit will spoil you for anything else.

Before complaining of insomnia, try increasing your thread count to three hundred.

Ceiling fans and swaying indoor palm trees make you feel like you're living in colonial splendor.

Clear your mind with this simple meditation

Experience the magic of...

Find your balance.

fresh-squeezed iced tea with mint leaves

Her sunny disposition had a way of putting nervous coworkers at ease.

His aftershave lotion felt crisp and bracing.

"I took my junior year off to go find myself."

"In this world without quiet corners, there can be no easy escapes from history, from hullabaloo, from terrible, unquiet fuss." (Salman Rushdie)

Indulge yourself.

Let our concierge secure tickets for you, attend to your dry cleaning, or schedule a day at our luxurious spa.

One Hundred Years of Solitude (book by Gabriel Garcia Marquez)

Our natural mineral baths restore and heal.

Quiet your internal chatter.

revive

stolen moments

Surrender yourself to the surf and sand.

Tune it out.

"Visualize yourself at a beach. Hear the waves pound against the shore."

"Will you join me on the veranda for a 6 p.m. pick-me-up?"

"You must learn to be still in the midst of activity and to be vibrantly alive in repose." (Indira Gandhi)

You time

your home away from home

LANGUAGE POLICE

You need to match the personality of your copy to the personality of the client company for whom you are writing, or the result will be disastrous. So before your copy goes off on some kind of new age Eastern philosophy jag, please double check the strategy with your client. (You always want your customers to nod their heads in recognition, not shake their heads from side to side, wondering what the heck the company's been smoking.)

5. It Makes a Statement

Never underestimate people's vanity or their tendency to identify with the products that they own. When someone purchases a product, that's a little piece of his personality on display for the whole world to judge. In the late 1980s, vanity reached its peak and there were logos screaming from every handbag, car hood ornament, and designer blue jean. During the early '90s, vanity went "underground" for a spell during a soft spot in the economy. But today, vanity is in again, although with less hardware to show (off) for itself. Ease up on the humor when you're trying to persuade someone that a particular product will reflect well on his station in life. Fashion statements tend to cost a fortune (you could buy a small country for less) and you don't want to inadvertently sell the generic version of the same product!

a coveted number of autographed copies

A long heritage of…

a sneak preview of _____'s most important collection

a thorough command of etiquette

Among Manhattan's privileged elite,

as seen in _____ (auction house) catalog

Celebrate your magnificence.

cell phones in custom colors

classic pleats

Connoisseurs have noted its floral tones with just a hint of spice.*

Cuban cigars

cultured pearls

designer baby carriage

dripping with diamonds

Ebony and ivory jewelry complements today's new black-and-white graphic motifs.

Every guest is treated like a celebrity.

fastidious attention to detail

fine filigree

flawless pedigree

hand-painted jeans

He had a dissipated look that hinted of too many late, liquor-filled nights.

Her biggest asset was her megawatt personality.

Her schedule was grueling: it was off to St. Bart's in the winter, St. Moritz in the fall, Aspen in the winter, and Southampton in the summer.

Her unique style was a little bit street, with some elements of runway and classic thrown in as well.

He's a poster child for Princeton University's writing department.

He's best friends with some of the richest and most influential people in the city.

His winsome smile was fatal. Even his competitors loved him.

If you've got 'em, flaunt 'em.

"I'm feeling haute, haute, haute."**

Impeccable manners are always in fashion.

It has a certain cachet.

It seemed like everyone was in Monte Carlo that fall—from Hollywood icons to heads of state to international business tycoons.

Its provenance is indisputable.

Limited edition watches range from $2,000 to $10,000. Important estate jewelry…

Looking as if he had stepped off the set of the movie *The Age of Innocence,* Lloyd…

Louis XIV first popularized Empire furniture.

Make an entrance. Wear flamboyant red for a change.

Meet the celebrities who are eager to dress you for your next gala.

meticulously tailored
monogrammed
- cuffs
- towels

one of the distinguishing characteristics...
one of the few genuine Renoirs on the market today
our exclusive made-to-order tassel loafers
polo player logos (Ralph Lauren)
power lunch
power shoulder pads
The 48 Laws of Power (book by Robert Greene)
recognized as one of the world's leading museums
Save the whales.
Save the world. Drive a hybrid***
select customers
Send a message. Tell your local congressman...
She always arrives fashionably late.
She had a face only a mother could love.
She put on airs.
signed by the artist
"Speak softly and carry a big stick." (Theodore Roosevelt)
Spread your wings.
sultry style, wrapped in romanticism
the Ferrari of _____
The high social season originally lasted from December 15 until February 23.
the investment boot

the leisured classes

The _____ pen. It makes a statement before you write a word

the place to see and be seen

The stately Georgian manor perches on the southern tip of the community's historic section.

The wait list for the _____ handbag is six months. But for a small group of select customers,

VIP lounge

vanity

- cases
- license plates
- publishing

world famous shopping and dining

You have arrived.

*For more "Words from Our Distinguished Wines and Spirits Collection," check out the Appendix.

**For more "Fashion-centric Words That Are Always in Fashion," check out the Appendix.

***For other "Rev It Up Car Words," check out the Appendix.

Word Jumble

Steep discounts and sudden availability could tarnish the way a customer views a brand. Long wait lists and "full retail price" is part of the allure of certain products, and removing these barriers may in fact depress sales. Remember Woody Allen's famous statement, "I'd never join a club that would allow a person like me to become a member." Nothing will knock a pricey brand off its pedestal faster than announcing that it's coming to a mall near you.

Product Attributes Exercise: You've got (junk) mail

Write a flyer for a yard sale.

Back when Aunt Zelda was alive, you loved her more than anyone on the planet. But now she has died and left you a large inheritance that you could have lived without—a moving van full of junk. The Empire-inspired bee motif drapes are indeed a curiosity…you're curious if the Salvation Army will consent to take them off your hands for free! Fortunately, taste is a completely subjective matter, and one person's hideous armoire is another person's cherished storage nook. Think about the benefits of some of Zelda's furniture. For one thing, all of it has endured. Are there any other product attributes you can find in the heap? Write your first draft on an uncluttered blank sheet of paper.

Product Attributes Exercise Cheat Sheet: 5 Phrases to Experiment With

1. Is it possible to go back in time?
2. You're not in college anymore. So how come your furniture still looks like it belongs in a dorm?
3. Nope, it's not available at Pottery Barn
4. It's hard to think outside the box when you're sitting on modular furniture
5. A touch of Victorian elegance in a pre-fab world

And 1 Phrase to Avoid, No Matter What:

Make me an offer on the whole lot! (You don't want to make poor Aunt Zelda roll in her grave.)

Section VII:
Conclusion: Edit, Edit, Revise, and Tweak

By now, you've mastered the basics of copywriting. You made it your cardinal mission to communicate your message above all else. You stuck to your strategy and feel confident that you've given your prospect a compelling reason to buy your product or service. You've eliminated unnecessary words and flounces. Your copy is so adjective-free that perhaps you've gone back and added an adjective or two just to keep it interesting.

It's now the magical moment when you can sit back and view your copy from a critical distance. Please take ten minutes right now, and subject your copy to this final test.

The Five W's of Writing Great Copy

1. **The "What."** What is your message? Can someone reading your prose condense your message into one core sentence? "I should buy seventeen thousand widgets from the XYZ company immediately."
2. **The "Why."** Why should your prospect do what you want her to do? Can she summarize your eloquent arguments in one additional sentence? "When CCT converted to the high-tech widget system, their sales tripled in just eighteen months. I want my sales to triple also." (Okay, that was two sentences.)

3. **The "Who."** In this case, the Who is YOU. Make certain that your copy sells your prospect on the notion of doing business with you—your product, your service, or you directly. You want your customer to be thinking, "I better get this woman over here to show me her widgets!" Remember that the last thing you want to do is convince a customer to go sample someone else's widgets, or to do business with someone other than you. That would be most disheartening.

4. **The "Wow!"** Is your prospect excited about doing what you recommend? Can she move the ball forward at her company with the materials that you've provided? Or do you need to arrange a special time to meet with her in person? If she needs to run your idea by someone else at her company, is she marching over to his office right now?

5. **The "When."** The When is today, within the hour, in the next two seconds, without delay. Double check your copy; and make sure that you've instilled a sense of urgency in your prospect. Hopefully, she can't wait to get started on your project NOW.

Does your copy pass this simple test? If you're having trouble with the What or the Why, go back and reread "The 12 Laws of Writing Compelling Copy." Above all, don't despair. Your copy has come a long way, and with some tweaking, it will be just brilliant. Do you feel like you haven't quite nailed the Who? This is critical, so by all means, review section VI, "Product Attributes." Again, you are being tough on your copy for a reason. You want it to work gangbusters.

If your copy is wowing you, have faith that it will impress others. If you feel like the Wow is—like, wow!—totally missing for some reason, review the section on making your copy provocative. Often, with just a simple fix, your copy will do exactly what you intend, which is to touch, inspire, amaze, and urge people to action.

When? Immediately, of course. If you have followed the advice in this book, hopefully your phone should start ringing off the hook before you've even finished reading this sentence.

How I Wrote the Appendix

Anyone flipping through this appendix will recognize that capturing every single word or phrase associated with a particular category is absolutely impossible. I tried not to let this deter me. Instead, I decided to view this appendix as a "collection." And just like a collection of cowboy boots, jewelry, or art glass, space for housing them is ultra limited. (If you happen to live in Manhattan, just think about your own closet space. If you don't, take my word for it—there's never enough space to collect all of the things that we love!)

Once I accepted this fact, I decided to embrace the limitations of the form, rather than letting them hold me back from the challenge. I began to view the appendix as a "time capsule" of words and phrases, with an emphasis on those that are absolutely current. As a whole, I anticipate that the appendix will serve as a thesaurus of words and phrases that will guide you in your business writing, right here, today, at this minute, in 2006. Come 2007, one or two of these words and phrases may be outdated, to be recycled down the road perhaps, like that perennial phoenix of fashion: the bell-bottom.

I deliberately put limits on each section—the way that one might conserve precious closet space—fifty words or simple phrases for the first thirteen lists in the Synonym Finder, unless the particular attribute genuinely merited a great deal more, in which case, I allowed myself a grand total of one hundred.

When I first started writing the industry-specific section of the Synonym Finder, I tried to tackle each collection in the same way, by crafting a basic, pared-down vocabulary list. But after several foiled attempts, I decided that the effort was utterly futile. Merely listing words wouldn't be all that helpful to you since you already know most of the words! Furthermore, when it comes to writing product copy, it's not the words, it's how you mix and match them that matters. This is the reason that the last five lists of the Synonym Finder are organized slightly differently, and why you'll find *both* words plus some more detailed phrases grouped here under several core concepts. Each of the lists for the Beauty, Diet, Car, Fashion, and Liquor industries contains one hundred words and phrases to help you in your quest for the big idea.

As you are skimming these lists, probably looking not for an exact phrase but for some simple inspiration, you may question why a particular word or phrase was omitted. The short answer: it was eliminated to create space for something smarter, savvier, or more relevant. But if you feel strongly that something significant was overlooked and you wish to write to me about it, my email address is: vicky@vickyoliver.com. I will do my best to include your entry in the revised edition of this book.

Meanwhile, my main focus in the months ahead will be to force myself to stop waking up at three o'clock in the morning, mumbling lists of words and phrases like a raving maniac, only to pull the manuscript out of my closet and discover that they were already included!

A friend of mine recently asked me, "How did you write this book, Vicky?" "That's not the question," I replied. "The real question is, 'Will I ever be able to *stop* writing this book?'" And the answer is: long after I have abandoned it for other books, with your input, this book will continue to write itself.

Appendix A: Synonym Finder

I. Artsy Words

Art

abstract expressionism
art deco
art nouveau
background
brushstrokes
canvas
caricature
cave paintings
chiaroscuro
collage
conceptual art
cubism
dabbler
dadaism
etching
fake*
• forgery
figurative
folk art
foreground
fresco
gallery showing
graffiti art
hieroglyphs
his _____ period
impressionism

_____-inspired

installation

landscape

light source

lithograph

masterpiece

minimalism

mobile

negative space

oil

Old Masters

opus

outsider art

oeuvre**

palette

pastel

perspective

photorealism

pointillism

pop art

portrait

primitive

provenance

school of _____

self-portrait

signed

silkscreen

stabile

still life

surrealism

symbolism

watercolor

woodcut

Architecture

baroque

blend in with the scenery

blueprint

clean lines

deconstructionism

draftsmanship

form follows function

gothic

modernism

postmodernism

rococo

the international style

Décor

art glass

base coat

Chinese lacquer

decorative painting

design solutions for Manhattan
    apartments

faux stone finish**

feng shui

flat color

geometric

gold leaf

granite counters

graphic

hand-painted

marbleized

metallic

mural

painterly

prints

rag-rolled

skim coat

spray painted

stencils

tapestries

textured

wallpaper

Sculpture

baroque

Early Middle Ages sculptures

religious artifacts

Romanesque

*See "Polar Opposites," in the Appendix.

**See "French Words That You Hear Bandied About," Section V, 13.

II. Cool Words

a player

amazing

awesome

Be More Chill (book by Ned Vizzini)

bohemian goddess

charming

classic _____ (insert name of the coolest person you know)

disarmingly warm and open

down-to-earth

dude magnet

dynamic

easy on the eyes

excellent

fiery

free spirit

friendly

full of vim and vigor

fun*

funky but chic

girl power

glammed up

got to have it

graceful

incredible

intense

kitschy**

laid back

like a fox

half uptown girl, half biker chick

high energy

hot

marches to her own drummer

100 percent herself

one-of-a-kind

original

outgoing

primo

quirky

rocker edge

self-confident

self-deprecating humor

self-esteem

spit fire

stylin'
the It accessory of the minute
too cool
'tude

turns heads and opens minds
unique
wacky

---

*See "Fun, Fun, Fun Words" in the Appendix.
**See "Yiddish That's Made Its Way into Spoken English," Section V, 13.

III. Exciting Words

a breathless ride

a frisson of surprise shot through him

a killer idea

a madcap adventure

adrenaline junkie

attention grabbing

blow me away

bracing

charismatic

controversial

drama queen (or king)*

edgy

electrifying

exhilarating

explosive

gets my mojo working**

gives me a charge

gives me goose bumps

hallucinogenic

invigorating

juicy

knocks your socks off

makes my spine tingle

mesmerizing

mind-bending

mind-blowing

nervy

on tenterhooks

provocative

pulsating

racy

rollercoaster mood swings***

rousing

scary

sensational

smoking (or just "smoke")

stimulating

stirring

stressed out***

take no prisoners

temptress

the buzz

the razor's edge

theatrics

thrill seeker
thrilling
titillating

turbocharged
waiting with baited breath
"You rock me."

*See "Today's Words vs. Yesteryear's Words," Section V, 4.

**See "Euphemisms" for *lust,* Section V, 6.

***See "Words That Get You in the Mood (Not *That* Mood)" Section V, 14.

IV. Words That Are Beyond Fabulous

"a champagne bubble of a girl"
    (*Bergdorf Blondes*, book by Plum Sykes)
a great catch
a hip ensemble
a hottie
a joy to do business with
a knockout
a trip
absolutely fabulous
adorable
adventuress
alluring
amazing
an innate sense of style
appealing
awesome
beautiful and brainy
bewitching
beyond
beyond the beguine
bootylicious
breathtaking

can take her home to Mom
captivating
Casanova
causes heart palpitations
celebrity
charismatic
cool*
divine
drop-dead handsome
enchanting
exquisite
exuberant
famous
fantastically maintained
fetching
finesses her way through every
    situation with ease
five-star
four-star
gifted
glittering
gorgeous, but obtainable

Grand Dame of _____

He captures the imagination and
    doesn't let it go.

He was really good.

hot

hot, sexy mama

huggable

hunk

hunk of burning love

impressive

ingénue of the moment

inspiring

intrinsically interesting

IT-girl

like a great, big teddy bear

like the girl next door

likeable

makes a statement

makes strong men shiver

my dream

object of desire

old world elegance

one of the most extraordinary per-
    formances that I have ever seen

ooh-la-la

oomph factor

over and above

phenomenal listener

pretty

ravishing

riveting

shimmering

simply irresistible

smart and sharp

spectacular

star power

star studded

stirring

striking

stunning

surpassed my expectations

sparkling

the diva

the pineapple of politeness

"therapized"

There was a certain sauciness about
    her that…

36-24-36

too fabulous for words

toothsome

totally sexy
trend setting
two thumbs up
unforgettable
unstoppable
Va Va Voom!
"What a humma."
whoa!
winning
wow factor
You've got what it takes.

*See "Cool Words" in the Appendix.

V. Free Words

As a gift from us,

As a special bonus,

As a token of our esteem,

benefits

• "benies"

extra

financially independent

-free

• alcohol-free

• cell-free zone

• duty-free

• hands-free

• nicotine-free

• scot-free

• sugar-free*

free and clear

• The mortgage was paid off years ago.

free as a bird

free-for-all

• no chains

• no holds barred

• The gloves have come off.

free month

free subscription

free trial offer

freebies

gift bag

goodies

grab bag

It's payback time.

no capital gains tax

no

• fines

• hidden costs

• liens

• penalties

• restrictions

• strings

• taxes withheld

• VAT

pays for itself

perks

Skip the first payment.

tax

• advantaged

• amnesty

- deferred
- free
- relief

The _____ is yours to keep,
    regardless.

Your money's working for you. Not
    Uncle Sam.

zero
- calories*
- dollars down
- nada, zed, zip

*See "Words to Diet for" in the Appendix.

VI. Fun, Fun, Fun Words

Born to shop. Forced to work.

Bright Lights, Big City (book by Jay
    McInerney)

Bring the whole gang.

campy

carefree

extravaganza

family-style entertainment

festive

fling

flirty

For a good time, call _____.

gone fishin'

good

• old days

• times

great escapes

happy reading

Have an adventure.

He tomcatted his way up the
    Eastern seaboard.

hilarity

joyride

Kick back and relax.

• daydream

• Do nothing.

• Laugh, play, share, unwind.

• Recharge your batteries.

Let your inhibitions go.

Let's rock.

Life, Sunny Side Up

noisemakers and party hats

out on the town

pizzazz

rollicking

romp

She's a live wire.

Take a walk on the wild side.

The Hitchhiker's Guide to the Galaxy
    (book by Douglas Adams)

the mating dance

the perfect spot to wine, dine, explore,
    and rediscover each other

thrill seeking*

• barefoot waterskiing

- base jumping
- bungee jumping
- cave diving
- parasailing
- trapeze flying
- Xtreme sports

Tonight's the night.

witty banter

- light, engaging repartee
- the lost art of conversation

*See "Exciting Words" in the Appendix.

VII. Super Intelligent Words

aces tests without studying for them

aptitude

articulate

breezed through Harvard

brilliant

cerebral

clever

culturally literate

egghead

800 on his SAT

enlightened

expert*
- encyclopedic knowledge
- proficient

genius

gifted

high performer

honed his brain muscle

IQ over 130

intellectual
- equal
- superior

know
- attain mastery
- educated
- know-it-all
- know it backwards and forwards
- know it inside out
- in-depth understanding
- informed
- versatile
- well-schooled in

maestro

Mensa Club

photographic memory

quick
- on the uptake
- witted

razor sharp

Renaissance Man (or Woman)

sparring partner

street smarts

the thinking man's _____

top 1 percent

top percentile

whiz

wise

wise to

- can't put one over on him
- in the loop

*See "Polar Opposites" in the Appendix.

VIII. New and Improved Words

beautified

Crews of workmen spiffed up the exterior.

edited

enhanced

Every room has been redecorated.

grand reopening

He cleaned up City Hall.

_____ had a facelift.

had some work done

makeunder

more inner pockets to help you stay organized

new
  • aerodynamic styling
  • state-of-the-art cataloging system

nipped and tucked

noodled with

now equipped with a V-6 engine

now in a new, flattering cut

now in every color of the rainbow

Our engineers started with a completely blank slate and...

overhauled the engine

polished

rebuilt

reconstructed from stem to stern

redesigned from the inside out

refined

refreshed

reinvented

remodeled

renovated

reorganized

repositioned

restructured

retooled

revamped

revitalized

revved up

She looks so good that she's positively unrecognizable.

spruced up

streamlined

subtly enhanced with

There's now an entire building devoted to math and sciences.

tougher than ever

transformed

tweaked

We cleaned the statue, making it look as good as new.

We listened to what you had to say and made some changes.

We put together a think tank of the best and brightest minds and they told us...

We refurbished the lobby of the hotel, returning it to its former splendor.

We replaced every brick in the old façade.

We rewrote the rules.

IX. Solid as a Rock Words

a bastion of calm
a calming force
a stand-up guy
a steady hand
boat analogies
- an anchor
- Don't rock the boat.
- port in a storm
- won't make waves

common sense
cool, calm, and collected
cool-headed
- "If you can keep your head when all about you / Are losing theirs and blaming it on you" ("If," poem by Rudyard Kipling)

dependable
direct
even-keeled
fair
feet planted firmly in the ground
firm footing
good judgment

grounded
- in reality
- in the facts

I ran it up the flagpole, and everyone loved it.
integrity
judicious
just
no-nonsense
poised
professional*
prudent
rational
realistic
reliable
rock-solid
sane
secure**
- emotionally
- financially

self-reliant
sober
sound (ideas or judgment)

steady

team player

the "go to" guy

trustworthy

unflappable

unpretentious

unshakeable

upstanding

We're behind you.

• We've got your back.

---

*See "Words That Interviewers Love," Section V, 1.

**See "Polar Opposites" in the Appendix.

X. Quick Words

automatic

breakneck

breathless

dash off

electric

energetically

fast turnaround

get a move on

hell-for-leather

impulse purchase

It ain't exactly brain surgery.*

It's a breeze.

It's a snap.

It's as easy as one, two, three.

It's easy.**

It's not rocket science.*

It's right at your fingertips.

It's within easy reach.

jamming

lickety split

lightening speed

mentally quick

• alert

• bright

• clever

• eagle-eyed

• intelligent***

• keen

• sharp-witted

navigate with ease

on demand

Personal Velocity (book by Rebecca
Miller)

prompt

pronto

race against time

rapid-fire

Rat Race*

Reordering is fast online.

Snap to it.

Sorry to eat and run.

speedy

• soar

• sprint

spontaneous

Step on it.

streaming video

swift

up and running in no time

We'll rush you your order.

You're just one click away.

*See "Business Slang," Section V, 13.

**See "Polar Opposites" in the Appendix.

***See "Super Intelligent Words" in the Appendix.

XI. The Seamy Underbelly of Modern Technology

Big Brother is watching you.

booting-up time

brainwashing

breaking into someone's email

burnout

"Can you please talk me through the problem?"

computer bugs
• crashes
• downtime
• glitches
• viruses

copycat attacks

copyright infringement

depersonalization

downloading
• movies illegally
• music illegally

dystopia

email flaming

Everyone's working 24/7.

gobbledygook code

hacking

hardware companies describing products as solutions

"I can't open your file. Can you please resend?"

identity theft
• phishing

If you aren't part of the solution, you're part of the problem.

Internet porn

lack of reliability and security

marketspeak

My computer caught a virus.

My computer's on the fritz.

My printer's jammed.

nations of robots

no boundaries

overload

piracy issues

planned obsolescence

pop ups

servers are down

spam

spyware

technobabble

terrorist attacks

vendors speaking in a language that we can't understand

video game addiction
video surveillance cameras clocking your every move
waiting for dial-up to kick in
worms that infect PCs
"You're breaking up! Call me back."

XII. Colors

Red

bordeaux

burgundy

coral

crimson

fire engine red

garnet

lollipop red

maroon

Mars red

pomegranate

poppy

rose

rouge

ruby

scarlet

Orange

blood orange

burnt orange

cantaloupe

carrot top

cheddar cheese orange

copper

harvest moon

peach

prison orange

pumpkin

sunset

tangerine

tequila sunrise

> **Word Up**
> Christo's 2004 art installation in Manhattan's Central Park sparked an intellectual debate about whether the color of fabric hanging from "The Gates" was saffron, "Home Depot Orange," or "Nedick's Orange." (Saffron is the yellow color of a spice used in rice dishes.)

Yellow

ash

butter

canary

egg yolk yellow

flaxen

gold

honey

jaundiced

lemon

medallion yellow

platinum

saffron

sun-washed

urine yellow

Green

acid green

aqua

avocado

chartreuse

citrine

emerald

four-leaf clover green

grass

jade

kelly green

mint

olive

pea soup green

sea sage

shamrock green

Blue

azure

baby blue

cerulean

cobalt

Dutch blue

IBM blue

lapis lazuli

midnight blue

navy blue

ocean blue

Old Glory Blue (color of blue on the
    Texas flag)

royal blue

sea

sky blue

star sapphire

turquoise

Indigo

blue heaven
blue jean blue
blue lagoon
blue-purple
blue-violet
blueberry
denim blue
French blue
periwinkle
ultra marine

Violet

amethyst
boysenberry

eggplant
eyes like Elizabeth Taylor's
grape
hyacinth
lilac
magenta
mauve
mulberry
royal purple
petunia
pixie dust
plum
purple
thistle
wisteria

Word Up
Give your colors a makeover. White is also "alabaster." Black is "ebony." And beige is "elephant's breath."

XIII. Genres

Book Genres

autobiography

biography

chick lit

diary

epistolary

flash fiction

graphic novel

hen lit

memoir

mystery

personal narrative

poetry

porn

• literary erotica

potboiler

romance

science fiction

senior lit

serious fiction

spy/thriller

travelogue

women's literature

Movie Genres

adult cartoon

adventure

animated

art film

biography

biopic

blockbuster

Bollywood

comedy

coming of age story

concert film

cult film

date movie

documentary

epic

fantasy

foreign film

graphic novel

Hollywood

horror

independent

James Bond

melodrama
mockumentary
mystery
period piece
porn
 • soft porn
road movie
roadie film
rockumentary
romance
romantic comedy
sci-fi
shoot 'em up
silent film
sit-com
space odyssey
spaghetti western
talking heads
tear jerker
thriller
western

Music Genres

anthem
bebop

big band
bluegrass
blues
bop
boy band pop
bubblegum
choral
classic rock
classical
cool jazz
country
country rock
crossover country
disco
Dixieland
girl band pop
gospel
Gregorian chant
heavy metal
hillbilly
hip-hop
house music
marching band
metal head rock
new age

pop	rock and roll
punk	rock opera
R&B	rockabilly
ragtime	soul

Word Up

Do you want to keep your finger on the pulse of cultural literacy? Count how many words are devoted to a topic. It's interesting to note that there are twice as many words to describe movie genres as book genres, even though roughly half of the movies made today started out as books first (rather than screenplays). And that's not even counting all of the genres that we attribute to individual directors, such as "Quentin Tarantino films" and "Robert Altman movies." Also, pay attention to movies that break a certain genre and then become their own genre, such as "Thelma and Louise movies."

XIV. Isn't She Lovely? Beauty Words

anti-aging

- ageless
- Doubletake. Can you tell the mother from the daughter?
- Go back in time.

    Fight gravity's pull.

    Fight the ravages of time.

    Fight the telltale signs of aging.

    makes tiny lines and crow's feet vanish

    Restore a more youthful looking you

    She's forty, going on twenty-five.

    Ten Beautiful Reasons to Go Back to Your Roots

    Turn back the clock.

Beauty comes from within.

Beauty is in the eyes of the beholder.

Beauty is only skin deep.

Bronzed Beauties Reveal Secrets of the Self-Made Tan

brow beat

- How to Arrive at Your Perfect Shape

cheeks

- How to Create the Illusion of Cheekbones

Editor's Picks

electrology

eyes

- Apply one coat of mascara, curl lashes, repeat.
- Smoke Gets in Your Eyes

_____'s flirty, feline look can be accomplished by...

For a beautiful Brazilian bikini wax without the pain...

hair problems and solutions

- big hair
- Celebrity Cuts
- chunky highlights
- curlers
- damage control
- How to Tame Those Bad Hair Day Dis-tresses

    flat iron

    Frizz Out

    hat hair

    In Search of the Perfect S Wave

- ingrown hairs
- Put moisture back in your hair.

    quench your hair

    revive dull, sun-fried locks

- scrunchies
- So you hate your hair.
- tousled bedroom hair
- weaves
- your mane

How to Act Like a Model (Or Just Look Like One)

If you want to know a woman's age, look at her hands.

It starts working immediately.

lips

- Liner adds staying power to lip color.
- lover's pout
- Pair bold eyes with a soft, neutral mouth.
- Pick your best feature—eyes or lips—and emphasize it.

manicures

- fake nails
- French
- frosted
- nail tattoos
- oval
- regular
- short for summer
- square

neck

- Look like a swan instead of a chicken.

Plastic surgery

- Do we all just want to look like china dolls?
- nip and tuck
- Real or Fake? _____'s Experts Weigh in (Check the answers below.)
- *The Stepford Wives* (movie)

philosophy

- "A woman's always younger than a man at equal years." (Elizabeth Barrett Browning)

- "I refuse to admit that I am more than fifty-two, even if that makes my children illegitimate." (Lady Nancy Astor)
- "I'm not interested in age. People who tell me their age are silly. You're as old as you feel." (Elizabeth Arden)
- "You can only perceive real beauty in a person as they get older." (Anouk Aimee)

professional styling tools

Skin Rx

- advanced restructuring serum
- Avoid products containing alcohol if your skin tends to turn red.
- dermabrasion
- dermatologist-recommended
- drink water
- Fight cellulite.
- firming action
- Five Essential Items Every Woman Needs to Look Her Best
- flawless finish
- help for combination skin
- laser
- lifting serum
- Love the Skin You're in
- makes blotchiness disappear
- Makeunder: During Summer's Hot, Sticky Days, Less Is More
- Mix your foundation with moisturizer for a dewy glow.
- Products with caffeine perk up tired skin.

- rehydrate your skin
- Seeing Red? Here's How to Calm Rosacea's Ugly Hue
- shine control
- T-zone
- targets problem areas
- The first foundation that's custom-matched to your exact skin color
- Wash with a loofah.

spa

- Paraffin wax treatments soften hands.

teeth

- Hollywood White. What Your Dentist Doesn't Want You to Know
- It takes fewer muscles to smile than to frown.

The "Before" shouldn't look better than the "After."

XV. Rev It Up Car Words

aerodynamics

attributes

- absolute quiet
- all-wheel drive
- alloy wheels
- can't feel the road
- compact
- designed for drivers of all shapes and sizes
- folding seats
- front-wheel drive
- jewel headlights
- off-road ground clearance
- perfectly weighted, laser-accurate steering
- rear-wheel drive
- roomier
- sleek
- smoother ride—"It's like driving your sofa."
- suspension
- tight turning radius
- towing capacity
- wider

bells and whistles

- air-conditioned glove compartment—keeps drinks frosty
- can move the seats around

- custom colors
- fancy racing stripes
- GPS navigation system—Guys never have to ask anyone for directions again.
- heated seats
- outfitted with a satellite radio

clones

- All of these models, the _____, the _____, and the _____are basically identical, except for the level of standard features.
- The _____ and _____ versions of this SUV are like fraternal twins. They're almost the same with a few distinct differences.
- The architecture was lifted from the…
- The _____ is simply a more fully equipped _____.

crossover

econobox

_____'s engineers went back to the drawing board, and…

fully loaded, with a long list of comfort and convenience extras, such as…

horsepower

- _____ adds more prancing hooves, and a thoroughbred is born.
- More Horses in _____'s Stable
- _____ satisfies horsepower junkies.
- Soup it up to one hundred horses.
- The _____ puts forty more horses on the ground.

hybrids

- a welcome alternative to those gas-guzzling SUVs
- Many SUVs are pretentious, overweight, and enormously wasteful. A

symbol of conspicuous consumption that...
- Now that oil is $60 a barrel...
- The _____ gets fifty-three miles to the gallon.
- You'll get better mileage, plus it runs a lot cleaner.
- You'll spend a lot less at the pump.

lineage
- All great sports cars have a racing heritage.
- The _____ has an impressive pedigree.

looks
- a thoroughbred bloodline and a purity of execution make the _____
- Although you won't find yourself fantasizing about _____'s sexy curves,
- Bigger is not always better. Sales of big SUVs tumble 6 percent this year.
- bulging bodywork and plus-size tires
- In Major Makeover, _____ Gets Smaller Nose and Tighter Rear End
- It's a cross between a _____ and a _____.
- It's big. It's plodding. It's ungainly. Is the new _____ the next dinosaur?
- Long and lean, the _____ has a sexy, toned physique.
- nice treads
- The exterior is more restrained and subtle, a nod to enthusiasts who'd rather drive than constantly be stopped for speeding.
- To lovers of the old _____, the new model's dashboard is heresy.
- With an uninspired brown-on-beige interior, poorly designed armrests, and sticky vinyl dashboard, the _____ is a lot like a cheap suit. It may see you through an emergency, but...
- With its burled oak, soft stitched leather, and ahead-of-the-curve CD system, the

inside cabin resembles a cocoon.

luxury

- American walnut, supple leather, and a metallic finish
- cruise control
- four-door
- From the grille to the resplendent paint job, _____ promises...
- leather steering wheel
- opulent splendor

performance

- high performance without the punishment
- hugs the corners
- In the Luxury Sport Utility Vehicle category, the _____ tops the charts.
- muscle car
- supercharged
- The _____ delivers this performance effortlessly.
- torque
- turbocharged
- V-8 engine
- V-12 engine
- zero to sixty in _____

ratings

- _____ finally flexes its muscle with...
- Its style is purely functional, but its commitment to practicality is an inspiration.
- The _____ combines vivid acceleration, purring engine sounds, and

velvet handling.
- The _____ is a staggeringly fast, marquee _____, powered by ____

room for seven to nine passengers (including your dog)

safety issues
- airbags
- anti-lock brakes
- Buckle up.
- Most drivers have no idea how to handle the roundabout.
- tire pressure alerts
- warranty

storage space
- _____ cubic feet of cargo room

Take her for a spin.
- Come in for a test drive.

XVI. Words to Diet for

A diet including fish, vegetables, almonds, garlic, chocolate, and red wine
can lower your risk of heart disease.
A Quick, Easy Way to Lose Ten Pounds: Wear Black
a spike in appetite
"After a certain age, you can have your face or you can have your ass—it's one
or the other. I have chosen my face, and I can just sit on the rest of it."
(Meryl Streep, quoting Catherine Deneuve)
After three years of non-stop dieting, I reached a plateau.
An integrated routine, designed to increase metabolism, burn fat, and build
strength starts with...
Are your meds making you fat? (No wonder you feel so depressed!)
"At two hundred sixty pounds, I felt like the Invisible Woman"
Atkins-friendly
binges
burns calories faster
burns fat, not muscle
Buy jeans one size smaller, and keep trying them on till they fit.
Caffeine and spicy foods may aggravate hot flashes.
calorie counter
carb-free
Coffee won't bust your diet (as long as you lay off the sugar and cream).
contains good cholesterol, not bad cholesterol
Control your portions or they will control you.

Could your thighs use a shrink?

diet du jour

Dieting Through Your 20s, 30s, 40s, 50s, 60s, and Beyond

diets

- *Sugarbusters Diet* (book by H. Leighton Steward, Morrison Bethea, MD, Sam Andrews, MD, and Luis Balart, MD)
- the Grapefruit Diet
- the "No Fast Food" Diet
- *The South Beach Diet* (book by Arthur Agatston, MD)

Do you have a love/hate relationship with your scale?

Drink eight glasses of water a day.

eases the pangs of carb withdrawal

Eat anything you want in moderation.

Eat like a king in the morning, a prince in the afternoon, and a pauper in the evening.

Eat when you're hungry; don't eat when you're not.

Exercise can help relieve moodiness as your body adjusts to life without nicotine.

fat

- burning
- farm
- free
- trimming

Feel full sooner. Eat more slowly.

Feel the burn.

Here's the skinny on...

hidden calories

Housework can burn up to three hundred fifty calories a day.

"I lost forty pounds and kissed plus-sizes goodbye"

"I lost one hundred ten pounds in six months" (Results not typical.)

"I started eating more fruits, veggies, whole grains, and lean meats"

"I was a closet eater. I used to hide jelly beans in the apothecary jars in my bathroom, and..."

Identify emotional eating.

Is a sedentary lifestyle causing your weight problem?

Is 125 pounds your "magic number"?

Keep a food diary.

Learn to love your mirror.

lightly seared, not fried

liposuction without surgery

Listen to your body.

Lose a size by summer

Lose fourteen pounds a year. Drink 1 percent milk instead of whole milk.

Lose the guilt

low fat, high fiber content

makes the cravings go away

Metabolism Slows Down During Menopause. Here's How to Start It Up Again

My Big Fat Greek Wedding (movie)

"Once I gave up fast food, the weight just slid off"

one calorie

One glass of white wine has seventy calories and under two grams of carbs.

no
- artificial sweeteners
- butter
- hydrogenated oils
- sodium
- sugar
- trans fat
- vegetable oils
- visible panty lines

People who eat salad before dinner eat 7 percent fewer calories during the meal.

Push through your weight plateau with these six easy steps.

Regular exercise can help you keep the weight off.

self-control*

substitute
- mixed green salad for Caesar salad
- mustard for ketchup
- six pieces of cucumber roll for six pieces of spicy tuna roll
- turnips for potatoes

speeds up your metabolism naturally

sugar-free

suppresses
- appetite
- cravings
- urges to snack after midnight

the pendulum swings back

33 percent of Americans are obese. Only 10 percent of the French are.

To stave off osteoporosis, try to walk, jog, dance, or jump rope three times a
week.

trims inches from your hips

Walk it off.

Walking thirty minutes a day can burn up to two hundred calories.

Want better buns in three days? Here's everything you need to know about
cardio crunches.

weigh in

Weigh yourself just once a week.

wiggle room

You can eat meat or fish for dinner, but don't mix them with potatoes or rice.

Your body is a temple.

zero cholesterol

*See Polar Opposites in the Appendix.

XVII. Fashion-centric Words That Are Always in Fashion

Bergdorf Blondes (book by Plum Sykes)

beyond out

classic styles that have resisted the passage of time

- Boho
- Boudoir
- Hippie Chick
- Man-Tailored
- Monochromatic
- Resort Wear
- School Girl Chic
- The "First Lady" Suit
- The Military Look
- The Mod Look
- The Preppy Look

couture

Do's and Don'ts

- Do go undercover as a brunette if you're really a blonde.
- Don't flash your midriff unless it looks like steel.
- Don't let the hem of your dress peek out from beneath your coat's hem.
- Don't look like a bag lady.
- Don't lose so much weight that you look like a lollipop.
- Don't match your lipstick and nail color.
- Don't wear shoes that are lighter than the color of your pantyhose.

- Don't wear white in fall.
- If you're going to a fancy lunch, don't arrive looking like you just rolled out of your health club.

eye candy

fashion faux pas

fashion finds under $100

Fashion Is Fickle. Style Endures

fashion cities
- London, Milan, New York, Paris, Tokyo

fashion plates
- fashionista
- glitterati
- style icon
- Supermodel _____ was spotted at _____.

fashion philosophies
- "Fashion is a form of ugliness so intolerable that we have to alter it every six months." (Oscar Wilde)
- "Fashion is what you adopt when you don't know who you are." (Quentin Crisp)

fashion radar

glamorous

Hitchcock Blondes

Holiday Season How-to: Go From the Office to a Party in Five Minutes Flat

house of _____

If you haven't worn it in three years, toss it.

Insider Secrets: How Celebrities Develop Their Own Styles

investment pieces
- A-line skirts
- black pumps
- cardigan sweaters
- structured jackets

knockoffs
- Buy the real thing or just look like you did.

lists
- fashion's A-listers
- the best-dressed list
- the worst-dressed list

Make a statement.

makeup zeitgeist

retro styles of yesteryear*
- blouses
  - cropped T-shirts
  - leopard velour tops
  - the poet's blouse
  - the ruffled look
  - tie-dyed shirts
- dresses
  - dresses over pants
  - muumuus
  - the coatdress

- pants
  - bell-bottoms
  - hip huggers
  - low riders
  - the pants suit
- skirts
  - maxi skirts
  - reversible
  - the wrap skirt
  - ultra-suede
  - uneven hemlines
- shoes
  - Mary Janes
  - patent leather
  - T-straps

Pink Is the New Black

Reinvent Your Look. Sixteen Experts Show You How

signature

Six Wardrobe Fixer-Uppers

so last season

splurges

the fabulous people behind the scenes

- fashion editors
- makeup artists
- photographers

- prop assistants
- retouchers
- style makers and trend spotters
- stylists
- up-and-coming designers

vintage junkie

what's hot**

- _____ are having a moment
- as seen on the catwalk
- seen on the runways from _____ to _____
- the must-have _____

*See "Today's Words vs. Yesteryear's Words," Section V, 4.
**See "Polar Opposites" in the Appendix.

XVIII. More Words from Our Distinguished Wine and Spirits Collection

aperitifs
 • dry vermouth
booze cruise
Cleanse your palate, swish the wine around in your mouth, and spit out.
cooking wine
decant
dessert wine
digestif
 • brandy, grappa, or port
hard liquor
 • gin
 • rum
 • scotch
 • tequila
 • vodka
hot rum toddy
How to Read a Wine Label
Irish coffee
Let it breathe.
liqueurs
 • Amaretto (almond)
 • Crème de menthe (mint)
 • Kahlua (coffee)
liquid lunch

mixed drinks
- apple martini
- cosmopolitan
- fuzzy navel
- mai tai
- margarita
- mojito
- piña colada
- rum 'n' Coke
- screaming orgasm
- screwdriver
- southside
- tequila sunrise
- whiskey sour
- white Russian

1985 was a very good year for wine.

on the rocks

Pinot Grigio may soon be more popular than Sauvignon Blanc.

Popular labels, such as _____ and _____ get marked up many times
over since restaurateurs recognize...

red wines
- Burgundy
- Cabernet
- Meritage
- Merlot

shaken, not stirred

Sideways (movie)

straight up

take one part _____, mix two parts _____

Ten percent of Americans consume wine once a week.

The Lost Weekend (movie)

The most famous white grape in France's _____ region is...

Then it ages in oak barrels for _____ years.

What Your Drink Says About You

When a wine is produced in mass quantities, wine connoisseurs turn up their noses at it.

When I asked for a sparkling rose, the sommelier gave me a withering stare.

white wines

- Champagne
- Chardonnay
- Pinot Blanc
- Pinot Grigio
- Pinot Gris
- Riesling
- Sauvignon Blanc
- White Burgundy
- Zinfandel

wine descriptions

- a bouquet of floral aromas
- a lively acidity
- a long, penetrating finish
- a strong hint of leather
- a tangy, sprightly wine that goes with spring dishes, such as...
- black cherry and berry flavors

- boisterous*
- citrusy
- crisp and delicious
- delicate
- dry
- earthen and toasty
- fresh and lively
- fruity
- full-bodied and zesty
- In a taste test of over one hundred white wines from France, Italy, Germany, Spain, Australia, New Zealand, and the U.S.,
- In terms of mouthfeel, this Zinfandel has the consistency of…
- light-bodied
- Many top rosés are made using the saignee method.
- marked by attractive pear and apricot notes
- more robust than…
- notes of vanilla, oak, and pear
- silky, lush*
- soft, dry, and cherry-flavored
- spicy
- The judges at the _____ were unanimous.
- This simple, but wonderfully refreshing wine…
- This wine tastes best when paired with…
- vivacious

*See Polar Opposites in the Appendix.

Polar Opposites

I. Fake

bogus

charade

cubic zirconium

deceived

dishonest

disingenuous

disreputable

faking it

false

falsies

falsifying documents

• fake ID Card

• fake passport

falsetto

forgery

fraud

hoax

illegitimate

• bastard stepchild

insincere

lie

• According to the paternity test, he's not the real father.

• black lie*

• cheat

• falsehood

• fib

- hoodwinked
- white lie*

plagiarism

plastic surgery

playing mind games**

poser

ruse

scam

schemes
  - money-laundering scheme
  - numbers-running scheme

- pyramid scheme

surreal
  - dreamlike
  - mind-altering drugs
  - trancelike

tall tales

The Wizard of Oz (movie)

trompe l'oiel***

unreliable

unscrupulous

untrustworthy

---

* See "Colors" in the Appendix.

** See "Words That Get You in the Mood (Not *That* Mood), Section V, 14.

*** See "Artsy Words," Décor in the Appendix.

II. Authentic

wild goose chase

actual

blue blood

- came over on the Mayflower
- Daughters of the American
  Revolution (DAR)

Candid Camera (TV show)

certified

facts

- cold, hard facts
- just the facts
- it's a fact

Evidence reveals:

faithful to

frankly

genuine

He gave his word.

- He vouched for it.

honest

honest-to-goodness

legitimate

no

- b.s.
- fine print
- magic bullets
- strings

on the up and up

plain English

proven

real

- feels so real
- get real
- the real deal
- *The Real World* (TV show)

reliable

reality check

reality TV

Sincerely,

solid*

straight

- from the hip
- scoop
- shooter
- story

- talk
- up

tells it like it is

tested by

- dentists
- kids everywhere
- moms

the truth is,

the unvarnished facts

valid

*See "It's Enduring," Section VI, 2.

III. Expert

a whiz

accomplished

aced every test with flying colors

area of expertise

- it's her thing
- métier
- strong suit

award-winning

been in the field forever

grew up in the field

invented

knows a lot about

- has it down cold
- know-it-all*

  He's forgotten more than he's learned.
  His scope of knowledge is breathtaking.
- He wrote the book on...
- hip to
- long on
- paid his dues

- she knows

  her stuff

  what's what
- the authority

masterminded

over _____ years experience

pioneered

professional

skilled

since _____

specialist

- author
- collector
- commentator
- connoisseur**
- consummate politician***
- counselor

  mentor
- critic
- guru
- maven
- pro

- pundit
- scholar
- "sexpert"
- teacher
- technical expert
    MIS guy
- Zen master

talented

- She's a major talent.

* See "Super Intelligent Words" in the Appendix.

** See "More Words from Our Distinguished Wine and Spirits Collection" in the Appendix.

*** See "Business Slang," Section V, 13.

IV. Novice

amateur

babe in the woods

barely out of diapers

beginner's luck

blank slate

brand new to this whole _____ thing

dabbler

dilettante

fledgling

freshman

hobbyist

ignoramus

immature

inexperienced

jack of all trades, master of none

learning the ropes*

lightweight

neophyte

new kid

 • in school

 • on the block

newbie

not proficient

 • borderline incompetent

 • bungling

 • careless

 • hack

  scribbler

 • needs a lot of hand-holding*

 • needs a swift kick in the pants*

 • needs computer training

only here because he has an uncle in the firm"

 • sloppy

  too many typos

 • uninspired

 • unqualified

out of his league

perennial student

raw

recruit

rookie

still "green"

The Apprentice (TV show)

The Graduate (movie)
trainee
training program
uncultured
  • lowbrow
undeveloped
wet behind the ears
virgin**

*See "Business Slang," Section V, 13.
** See "Sex Appeal," Section IV, 5.

V. Secure

emotional security

- confidence
- in perfect balance
  harmony
  yin-yang*
- in the womb
- in touch
  with reality
  with yourself
- no worries
  carefree
  "To sleep! perchance to dream"
  (*Hamlet* by William Shakespeare)
  You'll never doubt yourself again.
  Your mind is at ease.**
- Peace,
- relaxed
- safe harbor
  Any port in a storm.
- self-esteem
- self-reliant
- serene
- "therapized"

financially secure

- can make ends meet
- comfortable
- comfortably off
- established
- in the black***
- independently wealthy
- not lifestyle-challenged
- profitable
- retirement strategies
  401K
  marry rich
  nest egg
  Rainy Day fund
  Social Security
- rich****
  fabulously rich
  The *Fortune* 500
  well-heeled clientele
- solvent
- the fast track
- upper middle class
- You're in your peak earning years.

insulated

- in a bubble
- ____ takes the guesswork out of _____
- You're locked into a good rate, even if interest rates rise.

iron-clad protection

---

*See "It's So Refreshing (or Relaxing)," Section VI, 4.

**See "You Will Achieve Peace of Mind," Section IV, 4.

***See "Colors" in the Appendix.

****See "For Richer or Richer," Section IV, 2.

WORD UP

Blame it on the times. Signing off letters and emails with the word "Peace" has become almost as popular as closing with "Sincerely" or "Cordially." What's next, "May the force be with you?"

VI. Insecure

emotional insecurity
- a hazard to himself and others
- codependent
- crazy*
- dangerous
- delusional
- fragile
- hostile

    anger management issues
- needs constant reassurance
- needs many pats on the back
- needy
- paranoid
- unstable

financially insecure
- austerity budget
- bad credit rating
- bankrupt
- business went belly up
- can't make ends meet
- destitute
- dot com bust

- downtrodden
- fallen on hard times
- financial adversity
- hard up
- hitting up friends for cash
- in the red
- lost all his money
- maxed out the credit card
- no

    prospects

    financial cushion
- poor

    down and out

    down on his luck

    impoverished

    starving artist

    struggling
- unemployable
- unemployed

    in between gigs
- watching every penny

poorly made

- careless workmanship
- rickety
- seams showing
- shoddy construction
- unbalanced
- unsafe

*See "Words That Get You in the Mood (Not *That* Mood)," Section V, 14.

VII. It's Easy

cushy

easy on the eyes

easy to grasp
- It's a cinch.
- It's a no-brainer.*
- It's a piece of cake.
    effortless
- It's child's play.
- It's condensed.
    abridged version
- It's intuitive.
- It's simple.
- It's so easy to fall in love. Just tell us what you're looking for, and…
- It's straightforward.
- There are easy-to-follow instructions.
    clearly written pointers
    Directions in plain English guide you every step of the way.
    jargon-free tips
    step-by-step directions
- There's no learning curve.**
- There's nothing to memorize.
- uncomplicated
- user-friendly
    Just point and click.
    Mac and PC compatible
    There's nothing to download.
- You'll get it after one try.

easy to install
- Just pop our CD in your computer, drag the icon to your desktop, and… you'll be up and running in seconds.
- no downtime
- The mouse pad is built in.

easy to use
- ergonomically designed keyboard
- hands-free
- one touch and…

easy to wear
- no ironing
- reversible
- Slip into something comfortable.

- wrinkle-free

facilitates

- cuts through the red tape***
- greases the wheels
- lubricates
- paves the way
- unclogs the lines of communication

fewer steps

- back to basics.
- 2-in-1 ___ plus ____

Take it easy.****

*See "Quick Words" in the Appendix.
**See "Look Marge, How Convenient!," Section VI, 3.
***See "Business Slang," Section V, 13.
****See "You Will Achieve Peace of Mind," Section IV, 4.

VIII. It's Hard

hard-boiled

hard lessons

• the hard way

hard luck case

It's hard to grasp.

• hurting the brain

   a brain tease

   a brain tickler

   straining my brain

• I can't make heads or tails of it.

• I just don't get it.

• It's

   a conundrum

   a paradox

   a riddle

   awkward to say

   beyond confusing

   counterintuitive

   counterproductive

   difficult

   hard to get

   impenetrable

   impossible to understand

   mystifying

   puzzling

   taxing

   too much work for too little reward

hard on people

• bitchy

• hard-hearted

• hard to get along with

• hard to take

• heart turned to stone

hard surfaces

• granite

• in between a rock and a hard place

• "in like flint"

• marble

• rock hard

• steely gaze

• stone

hard to wear

• too tight

• unflattering

hard up (for cash)

hard year

- hardship

hard work

- hard labor (often physical)
- She's even harder on herself than she is on her people.
- She works hard for the money.*
- "The harder I work, the higher she
  tells me to jump."

---

*See "Word Up," Section I, 2.

IX. Self-control

confidence

grace under pressure

in control
- dispassionate*
- doesn't blab (people's secrets)
- doesn't spill (company secrets)
- follows protocols
- keeps his cool
    a "cool head"
    Stay cool.
- in command
- poker face

mastery
- doesn't get derailed easily

no
- obsessions
- problems with authority figures

organized

poise
- balance
- calming presence
- composure
- doesn't overreact to news, good or

bad
- equilibrium
- keeps emotions in check
- levelheaded
- never "loses it"
- not easily flustered
- reliable**
- restrained
- role model for others
- self
    - assured
    - contained
    - possessed
- stiff upper lip
- strong leadership abilities
- trustworthy
- understated
- unexcitable
- unperturbed
    unruffled
- unswerving

pragmatic
- highly functional

- predictable
- reasonable

stature

- presence of mind

stoic

*See "Words That Get You in the Mood. (Not *That* Mood)," Section V, 14.

**See "Solid as a Rock Words" in the Appendix.

X. Out of Control

angry*
- bent out of shape
- erupted
- exploded
- fuming
- having a meltdown
- heated
- hostile
- in
    a purple rage**
    an uncontrollable rage
- letting him have it
- livid
- "off the deep end"
- "on the ledge"
- outraged
- rabid
    foaming at the mouth
- seeing red**
- seething
- venting

chaos
- bedlam
- madhouse
- spiraling out of control
- swerving out of control
- "The inmates are running the asylum."

communication breakdowns
- communication blips
- snafus

disorganized

dysfunctional

off balance

The company isn't working.
- hiccups in the system
- no one's manning the controls
- no one's running the ship
- revolving door
- We're experiencing growing pains.

The government isn't working.
- anarchy
    civil disobedience
    riots
    unrest
- friendly fire

The system isn't working.
- All hell broke loose.
- crossed wires
- haywire
- misfires
- trying to put out fires

---

*See "Words That Get You in the Mood (Not *That* Mood)," Section V, 14.

**See "Colors" in the Appendix.

XI. What's Hot

all the rage

as seen on _____

au courant*

chichi

Fashion Avenue (a.k.a. 7th Avenue,
  Manhattan, New York)

finger on the pulse

hot places to be seen
 • after-parties
 • galas
 • hot spots
 • lounges
 • power
    breakfasts
    fests
    scenes

hip

in
 • beyond in
 • vogue

It's a happening.

on the

 • cutting edge
 • leading edge

on trend
 • trend spotting

people who know what's hot
 • beautiful people
 • café society
 • fashion elite
 • futurists
 • glitterati**
 • globe-trotters
 • Hollywood royalty
 • jet-setter
 • L.A.'s toniest women
 • man about town
 • smart set
 • socialites
 • super-rich elite
 • the darling of the _____ (insert
    French fashion magazine) set
 • the in crowd
 • today's tastemakers

- trendsetters
set the fashion
sign of the times
style-conscious
swanky
the new look
ultrastylish
What's
  - beyond in
  - new
  - new and noteworthy
  - the buzz?
  - the word?

*See "French Words That You Hear Bandied About," Section V, 13.
**See "Fashion-centric Words That Are Always in Fashion" in the Appendix.

XII. What's Not

antiquated

"Been there, done that."

beyond out

humdrum
- ho hum

irrelevant
- "doesn't even register on my radar"

lacking
- "oomph"
- the spark
- verve
- vision

out of touch
- He's a throwback to the time when...

outmoded

passé*

past it

people who aren't hot
- copycats
- dinosaurs
- fossils
- has-beens
- "He's a strange bird."

- "He's right out of central casting."
- mall rats
- never-weres
- "She's living in some sort of time warp."
- "the great unwashed"
- wannabes

personality-free

seen better days

so five minutes ago
- belated
- too little, too late
- yesterday's news

stale

style-challenged

the bourgeoisie

to be left
- behind
- in the dust

unappetizing

uncool (unless it becomes "cool" to be "uncool")

undistinguished

unfashionable
unimaginative
unimpressive
uninspired
unkempt
unmemorable
unoriginal
unremarkable
"Yawn."

*See "French Words That You Hear Bandied About," Section V, 13.

XIII. Boisterous

blustery
- braggart
- bravado
- bullying
- "cock of the walk"
- "full of sound and fury" (*Macbeth,* play by William Shakespeare)
- rollicking
- swaggering
- swashbuckling

excited
- clamorous
- exhilarated
- impassioned
- in a lather
- in a tizzy
- in an uproar
- restive
- stirred
- The natives are getting restless.
- wild
    -eyed

- worked up

loud
- bringing down the house
- cacophony
- commotion
- din
- flap
- fracas
- "Guys, can you please keep it down to a dull roar?"
- hubbub
- hullabaloo
- "I can't hear myself think."
- noise
- pump up the volume
- racket
- raise
    Cain
    your voice
- shouting to be heard above the noise
- thunderous applause

noisemakers

- bullhorns
- fireworks*
- honking
- toot

  your own horn
- trumpet calls

raucous

rowdy

whoop it up

*See "Sex Appeal," Section IV, 5.

Word Up
The word "noise" is derived from the Latin word "nausea." Coincidence? Not necessarily. Studies link random noise, such as car honking and blasting music, to increased stress, and even cardio-vascular disease. Think about it the next time you're tempted to pump up the volume.

XIV. Quiet

calm before the storm

composure

- achieve serenity
- quiet your inner voice
- transcendental meditation
- yoga

in repose

introspective

- quiet contemplation

peaceful

retiring

shy

silence

- Be considerate to the performers on stage. Silence your cell phones.
- cloak and dagger secrecy
  "Let's keep this confidential."
  Mum's the word.
  "Shut your mouth, girlfriend."*
  under wraps
- dead of night
- fall silent
  simmer down

- hush
- "Silence is golden." (The Bible)
- silken repose

"To sleep! perchance to dream"
  (Hamlet, play by William Shakespeare)

stagnation

- death
- motionless
- placid
- status quo
- stuck in a rut
- We're just marking time.

subdue

- break the fall
- censor
  muffle (criticism)
  muzzle (complaints)
  neutralize (all negative feedback)
- cradle
- cushion the blow
- lull
  him to sleep
  him into a stupor

- pacify
- suppress
- tranquilize
  - Have you had your meds today?

"The mass of men lead lives of quiet desperation." (*Walden,* book by Henry David Thoreau)

You could hear a pin drop.

*See "Valley Girlisms," Section V, 13.

XV. Silky, Lush

flowing
- floats
- lithe
- ripples
- skims your silhouette
- willowy

graceful

luxurious

opulent

plush

shiny
- gleaming
- glimmering
- glossy
- luminous
- luster
- reflects light
- satiny
- sheen
- shimmering
- slick

silk
-lined gloves
-screen printing
- sheets
- stocking district (Fashion Avenue, 7th Avenue, Manhattan)
- worm

sleek

slinky

smooth
- even
- flat
- fine
  -grained
  -spun
- refined
- supple
- uniform
- unwrinkled

soft
- caresses your curves
- delicate
- downy

- gauzy
- gentle
- on gossamer wings

The Silk Road

The Silk Trade (first developed in China sometime between 6000 BC and 3000 BC)

wild silk vs. cultivated silk

voluptuous

- sensuous

Word Up

Someone who is a "silk stocking" is a nobleman. Someone who works in the silk stocking district in Manhattan may be creating haute couture clothes for a nobleman.

XVI. Rough

rough textures
- bumpy
- bristles
- coarse
- corrugated
- crinkled
- crumpled
- dimpled
- exposed seams
- furrowed
- grainy
- harsh
- jagged edges
- leathery
- nonuniform
- nubby*
- pimples
- pockmarked
- rough-hewn
- scraggly
- shaggy
- stubble
    five o'clock shadow

- There may be some irregularities in the fabric.
- uneven
- wrinkled

uncivilized
- barbaric
- boisterous**
- boorish
- brusque
- coarse language
    crass
    crude, rude, lewd, and socially
    unacceptable
    indecent
    offensive
    politically incorrect
- gruff
- guttersnipe
- hick
- hillbilly
- ill-bred
- redneck
- raw

- "She's a bit rough around the edges."
- uncouth
- uncultured
- unrefined
- vulgar
- yokel

- You can't take him anywhere.

*See "Fashion-centric Words That Are Always in Fashion" in the Appendix.

**See "Boisterous," Polar Opposites in the Appendix.

XVII. Light

aura

beacon

blinding

brilliant

colors*

• cream

• ecru

• eggshell

• milk white

dawn

• "rosy-fingered Dawn" (*The Odyssey*, poem by Homer)

dazzling

fiery

flash

flickering

fluorescent

glare

glinting

glistening

glittering

glow

• worms

goddesses

• Luna (Roman goddess of the Moon)

• Selene (Greek goddess of the Moon. Selene was worshipped on the days of the full and new moons.)

halo

halogen

"I saw the light."

illumination

incandescence

Knight in shining armor

"Let there be light." (The Bible)

light surfaces

• ivory

• chandelier crystals

• diamonds

• gold

• porcelain skin

• silver

moonlight

resplendent

shimmering

shiny

sparkling

spotlight

sun

• Apollo

stroboscopic

To the Lighthouse
    (book by Virginia Woolf)

"the white radiance of eternity" ("Adonais,"
    poem by Percy Bysshe Shelley)

torch

x-ray

*See "Colors" in the Appendix.

XVIII. Dark

black
- comedy*
- list
- mark
- mood
- out
- sheep
- tie affair

cloudy

colors**
- caviar
- coffee
- ebony
- India Ink
- jet black
- mink
- raven
- pitch-black
- vamp

Dark
- Ages
- cloud hanging over him

- TV

  Buffy the Vampire Slayer (TV show)

  Charmed (TV show)

eclipse

embers

evil incarnate
- diabolical
- nefarious
- sinful
- *The Devil Wears Prada* (book by Lauren Weisberger)

funereal

Goth

heinous

kohl

mascara***

melancholy
- discouraged****
- disheartened
- dispirited

midnight

Satan

shade

shadows

"She wouldn't darken my door with
her presence."

squid ink

the Dark Side

vampires

witchcraft

- black magic
- the Wicked Witch of the West (character from *The Wonderful Wizard of Oz,* book by L. Frank Baum)
- voodoo dolls

---

*See "Genres" in the Appendix.

**See "Colors" in the Appendix.

***See "Isn't She Lovely? Beauty Words" in the Appendix.

****See "Words That Get You in the Mood (Not *That* Mood)," Section V, 14.

XIX. Miniscule

a pinch of

a soupçon of*

Baby (term of endearment)

childlike words for "minuscule"

 • eenie weenie

 • iddy biddy

 • itsy bitsy

 • teensie

dash

diminished

diminutive

dinky

dot

elfin

eye of the needle

granular

"He made me feel small."

infinitesimal

insignificant

Lilliputian

little

marginalize

matchbook apartment

micro

 - mini

 - scopic

miniature

 • poodle

 • schnauzer

minimize

minor

minute

narrow

petite*

petty

pinpoint

reduce

runty

scientific words for "small"

 • atom

 • cell

 • subatomic particle

 • quark

shrink

shriveled

smidgen

speck

Thumbelina (fairytale by Hans
    Christian Andersen)

tiny

  •Tiny Tim (character from *A Christmas
    Carol,* book by Charles Dickens)

tots

wee

*See "French Words That You Hear Bandied About," Section V, 13.

XX. Gargantuan

a bonanza

a Chinese menu of options

astronomical

Big (movie)

boundless

colossal

countless

encyclopedic

endless

epic

ever-expanding universe

exhaustive

exponential

extensive

font of knowledge

Hollywood blockbuster

humongous

"If you took all the people whose first names started with 'A,' and put them in a line, that line would stretch for…"

∞

interminable

jumbo

king-size

larger-than-life celebrities

macro

mammoth

massive

mega

monster

monumental

of biblical proportions

• Goliath

• the whale that swallowed Jonah

over the top

overwhelming

palatial

profuse

some big names starring in our collective fantasies

• Big Foot

• Hercules

• *Moby Dick* (book by Herman Melville)

- Paul Bunyan
- the beanstalk (from *Jack and the Beanstalk,* as told by Joseph Jacobs)

spacious

staggering

stupendous

there's no end in sight

titanic

whale (Gamblers who wage large bets are often called "whales.")

whopping

wide ride

vast

One List My Seventh-Grade English Teacher Asked Me to Include

Commonly Confused Words

Adverse: Opposing.
Averse: Disinclined.

Aggravate: To add to an already troublesome situation.
Irritate: To vex or annoy.

Allude: To refer to something indirectly.
Elude: To avoid.

Ante: Before.
Anti: Against, Opposed to.

Biannual: Occurring twice per year.
Biennial: Occurring every other year.

Bazaar: Market or a fair.
Bizarre: Weird.

Comprehensible: Understandable.
Comprehensive: Extensive.

Confidant: Trusted friend or advisor.
Confident: Sure of oneself.

Conscience: Sense of right and wrong.
Conscious: Aware.

Deceased: Dead.
Diseased: Ill.

Desert: To abandon.
Dessert: A course (generally sweet) that's served at the end of a meal.

Disinterested: Neutral, impartial.
Uninterested: Not interested in.

Emigrate: To leave a country.
Immigrate: To enter a country for the purpose of living there.

Enervate: To weaken or destroy the strength or vitality of.
Energize: To activate or invigorate.

Expand: To increase in size.
Expend: To spend (as in energy).

Fortuitous: It happens by chance or coincidence.
Fortunate: It happens by luck.

Hypercritical: Extremely critical, disapproving.
Hypocritical: Pretending to be virtuous.

Indigenous: Native.
Indigent: Needy.

Ingenious: Clever.
Ingenuous: Straightforward.

Official: Authorized.
Officious: Offering services that are neither wanted nor needed.

Persecute: To annoy or injure.
Prosecute: To press for the punishment of a crime.

Personal: Private.

Personnel: A group of people who work in a company or corporation.

Precede: To come before.

Proceed: To continue: to advance.

Restive: Contrary, resisting control.

Restless: Constantly moving, uneasy.

Veracious: Truthful.

Voracious: Having a large appetite.

Word Up

Commonly confused words are even more confusing when they are presented in a vacuum (such as on a list of Commonly Confused words!). That's because you're reading them out of context when the context could help to clarify their meanings. The real feat, however, is remembering that these words are easy to misspell when you're writing them in a sentence (because your computer's spell check function won't save you). Familiarity breeds facility, and with practice, you will become a pro at finding "le mot juste"—the perfect word.

Three Essays for Writers

If the doctor told me I had six minutes to live, I'd type a little faster.
—Isaac Asimov

How to Unblock Writer's Block (One Writer's Opinion)

You have a writing assignment that's due in three days. You dutifully sit down at the laptop in your office and begin typing. One hour later, you reread your lead and realize that it is indeed leaden. You write a completely different lead. It's even worse. You craft a third lead: it's dreadful.

You make a halfhearted attempt at a fourth lead. It's unspeakably bad. On the great writer's ladder of life, with rung one being matchbook copy and rung ten being Pulitzer Prize winning fiction, you're at rung negative five—*struggling to write an easy assignment.* Emotionally, you're teetering on the verge of extinction, somewhere between completely burned out and totally washed up. Lunch is in order. You decide to take a long, leisurely one.

Back at your desk, you take a deep breath, and reread your fifth lead. It makes you seriously consider a career in accounting. After all, accountants don't have to be all that creative. Just as you're musing about this potential career change—and how quickly you could get licensed to become a practicing accountant—your fifth lead ends up jamming the printer.

"Even my computer is blocked," you think with despair.

Writer's block often first coincides with the onset of a particularly challenging writing assignment, and the condition may persist from one day to several weeks. During this time, you can expect to accomplish no real work whatsoever. I have sat in countless writing classes where some writers have even claimed to be "blocked" for months on end—proving their assertions by showing up to class after class empty-handed. What causes otherwise productive writers to lay down their pens and become fallow? There are five main causes of writer's block:

1. You feel tired as hell
2. You're stressed out beyond belief
3. There's some mystery about the assignment that you don't understand
4. You have no ideas
5. Deadlines—you're either saddled with a completely unrealistic deadline for the amount of writing that's required, or, conversely, there's no deadline whatsoever.

Let's examine the root causes of writer's block to see if some might suggest simple treatments to the blocked state that all writers fear. But please note: *the best cure for writer's block is simply to start writing again.* So if the urge to write happens to strike while you're reading this essay, by all means, don't wait until you're sitting by your computer to indulge! Seize the moment: grab a pen and start scribbling some notes on any surface you can find—a nearby Post-it Note, the pages of your calendar, or even in the margins right here.

1. You feel tired as hell

Fact: If you have not been getting enough sleep, your brain ceases to function. Any writing effort that you expend after this point will be counterproductive. You have no choice but to stop writing until you have caught up on your rest. Don't feel guilty about it either. Recognize that walking away from your manuscript, direct mail copy, TV script, or storyboard right now is the best thing you can do for the assignment.

Leave the office early, and make it your mission to get the sleep that you require. However, if you have been running on empty for a while, ironically, you may find yourself far too exhausted to relax. If this is the case, try taking an over-the-counter, non-addictive sleeping aid for the next few nights until your brain feels like it's working again.

Above all, stop banging your head against a brick wall. Doing so really hurts, plus it's unlikely to make your copy sing. Take the time you need to recuperate and recharge. Your copy will reward you. And so will your boss (by not lighting a match to your copy).

2. You're stressed out beyond belief

Sleep deprivation contributes to stress. So do bad habits—like drinking too much alcohol, smoking too many cigarettes, having too much caffeine, or forgetting to exercise. On the other hand, if you have been working overtime for over a week in a pressure-cooker situation, you may need to take off early one night and sip a couple glasses of wine to ease the stress. Studies show that having two alcoholic drinks a night can reduce stress significantly. (But don't take up drinking if you've never done it before!)

If you generally live a vice-free life and still feel stressed out, it may be because you have too many commitments. Conversely, it could be because someone whom you care about deeply isn't nearly committed enough. Try taking a "time out" from ruminating about the problem. Multi-tasking just doesn't work when it comes to writing. Instead, vow to compartmentalize. When you're at the office, focus on the work. And when you're at home, give yourself permission to dwell on fixing your personal life. (If you're at work when the distraction occurs, make a deal with yourself to stop obsessing about the guy—or woman—for one full hour, and direct your mind on the writing task instead. You might create a private mantra for yourself such as, "I will write for one full hour, concentrating only on the task at hand, and then go back to worrying about the *jerk* later.")

Take a "mini vacation" from your stress and pick up your pen. Your stress will still be around once you've finished writing, but at least your mind will be clearer to deal with it!

3. There's some mystery about the assignment that you don't understand

Mysterious writing assignments often crop up in ad agencies, PR firms, and in-house advertising departments where someone in the vast chain of account service hasn't done her homework. Hence, you receive some emergency assignment where you're expected to write gripping copy without having all of the facts at your disposal. (Incidentally, while it's called an "assignment," this is really more like an exercise in futility.) You feel confused and annoyed, especially when you can't locate the one person who could answer all of your questions.

One sane solution is to approach your direct supervisor, explain the facts that you need to complete the task, and politely ask for an extension (so that you don't drive everyone crazy in your quest to unearth the information within the next few hours). Failing that, it often helps to do a bit of research on the project yourself. ("But that's not my job!" I can hear you shrieking. Believe me, I feel your pain, but consider: you could fritter away hours of angst waiting for the right person to return, time that's far better spent brushing up on the product details.)

Spend a couple of hours online. Look up the product, and try to answer your own questions! Then, email both your questions and the answers to the account person to double check the facts. This very step, which so many advertising copywriters fail to do, could be just the thing to tease out the real information that you need.

4. You have no ideas

Try not to panic! The most important thing is not to waste a lot of time writing up something until you are certain that you have an idea that's worth writing about. Instead of nervously watching the clock as it ticks down to "show time," go find someone at your company with whom you can brainstorm.

You might ask a more seasoned writer to help you knock around some ideas. If you work in a competitive environment where colleagues are reluctant to share their pearls of wisdom, don't be shy about asking your direct supervisor for help. Bosses frequently have *scores* of ideas that they never have time to commit to paper. You could end up picking up a "free idea" from your boss (which he will be even more likely to get behind because the idea was his to begin with!).

Do not add to the pressure by forcing yourself to turn in finished copy when you are struggling with idea generation. Instead, take all of the remaining time that you have for the assignment and use it to create a list of one-sentence core concepts. Crafting this list will take considerably less time than writing up an idea that you're not sure about. Worst-case scenario:

show up at the meeting with a list of thoughts, or even half-thoughts. One or two of them may spark a better idea from your boss or colleagues.

5. Deadlines

They're called "deadlines" because they can make you feel like you're going to drop dead from anxiety. If the deadline is completely unrealistic, do yourself a favor and don't commit to it in the first place. Instead, nicely promise your boss or client that you will do your best. Never promise any miracles if, in fact, you have doubts about being able to complete the assignment on time.

However, if the problem happens to be that you don't have a real deadline, by all means, make up one and stick to it. Deadlines (even the self-imposed kind) have a magical way of getting most writers over the hump of writer's block. So write down your deadline in both your calendar and on your daily To Do list, and start churning out that brilliant copy.

If you would like to share your thoughts with me about writer's block, feel free to email me at vicky@vickyoliver.com. But please, only write to me after you have completed today's writing assignment. The last thing I want to do is to encourage you to procrastinate on it for even one more second!

Welcome to Youtopia

In a perfect world, everyone would be paid to do what they were best at. Advertising copywriters, self-help book writers, TV production assistants, bullfighters, nurses, farmers, and venture capitalists would all receive equal pay because they would all be working for the common good.

Let's assume that, after a brief flirtation with bullfighting, you decided to become a copywriter. Every time that you wrote a piece of direct mail, everyone else would rush to open it. They would look forward to reading your superb copy, and be *thrilled* to learn interesting news about your product (something which would no doubt improve their already fairly perfect lives).

But until there's a Utopia, you'd be wise to master the rules here in plain old Youtopia, You.S.A. where things work a bit differently.

In Youtopia, some people are paid to do the things they love, some people are paid to do tasks they hate, and some people aren't paid anything, no matter how hard they try. So automatically, not everyone who opens your direct mail solicitations will do so in a happy, receptive state of mind. Some will even grumble about receiving too much junk mail (ingrates!) and toss your glorious copy without even glancing at it.

Salaries vary widely in Youtopia, which helps certain products and hurts others in this cutthroat, capitalist climate. For this reason, it's a good idea to step into your handy Youtopian Transporter Device at least once a week (the Ministry of Information gives them to copywriters for free), hit the "you" button, and take a quick journey deep inside your prospect's head.

What does your prospect do every day? How much money does he make doing it? What does he do when he's not doing it? Where does he eat lunch? Is he married or a complete commitmentphobe? Where does he hang out after hours? Is he an upstanding citizen of Youtopia? Or a rebel? What does he like to read? (Does he even have time to read?)

Once you map out the terrain inside the mind of your prospect, simply open a dialogue with him about how your product can improve his life. There are five tenets of Youtopian communication, which you would be wise to master.

1. Use the Word "You" a Lot
2. Flatter Your Prospect, but Don't Gild the Lily
3. Memorize the 7 (Un)Spiritual Laws of Success
4. Observe Youtopians in Their Secret Temples
5. Reach into the Cornucopia from Youtopia

Recognize that learning any new language takes some patience. (And no doubt about it, Youtopian grammar rules are a bitch.) But with practice, your communication skills will improve tremendously.

1. Use the Word "You" a Lot

Even though citizens of Youtopia are quite "me-oriented," they respond positively to the word "you." Position your product in a way that shows your target how he personally will gain from taking it into his life. Here are some you-oriented promises that work wonders:

- "You can become an expert in your field."
- "If you can find a wide panel TV screen for less money, I'll be happy to match the price."
- "Your kids will improve their scores by thirty points, or we will refund the full price of the class."
- "Imagine arriving at your college reunion a few pounds lighter than you were back in college."

You may become bored with using the word "you," but your prospects will never tire of hearing it, so sprinkle the word generously throughout your copy. Everyone loves to hear what you can do for them. Strive to become you-centric, and you will go far.

2. Flatter Your Prospect, but Don't Gild the Lily

In Youtopia, everyone is a celebrity in his own mind, with a thousand commitments a day (and feels far too stressed out to deliver on even half of them). For this reason, using some flattery works well. The language of flattery feeds the ego and makes prospects pause just long enough to listen to what you have to say. "You have been specially selected," "Only a handful of our best customers will receive this invitation," "It's a special reward for your loyalty," and "We would like you to become a member of the Inner Circle, a special group of customers whom we rely on to give us valuable feedback," are all promise statements designed to make prospects on Youtopia feel like V.I.P.Y.'s (Very Important Prospects of Youtopia).

However, always remember that in this land, narcissism runs rampant. In his own head, your prospect already believes that he *is* pretty special. And, after years of having his own self-love confirmed by marketers, he's wary of sycophants. Go ahead and use the flattery card, but don't max out on your preset spending limit (two compliments per letter, 2,500 compliments per lifetime limit), or else your prospect may tune out your words forever. (Your Flattery Card should have been included in your Youtopian Welcome Kit. If it's missing, please call 1-900-KISS-THEIR-BUTTS and punch in code 1234.)

3. Memorize the 7 (Un)Spiritual Laws of Success

Youtopian citizens live in a virtual world where technology morphs at warp speed. They have come to expect rapid change that is, generally speaking, for the better. Every week, Youtopians receive streams of data that are designed to help them upgrade and improve life in their pods—information that's delivered to them automatically via computer. Online turns out to be an excellent place for marketers to reach Youtopians. But there is a rhythm and pace to communicating with them there that you will need to embrace.

Recognize that the continuous change that is happening in Youtopia right now makes everyone feel like they're experiencing an eternal adrenaline rush. This makes them less inclined to spend any time at all with traditional advertising copy. In fact, now that the mass conversion to the Binary System has been successfully completed, no one has the patience to absorb any promises that are over two words long. However, this still gives you a lot of leeway. Here are seven product-focused sound bites that even the busiest Youtopians will respond to.

1. It's quick.
2. It's easy.
3. It's new.
4. It's cheap.
5. It performs.
6. It's good for him. (Okay, that's four words.)
7. It's fun.

Youtopians appreciate consistency. If you claim that a product is "quick," your description of it should also be a quick read. Ditto, especially, for point 7. The worst thing that you can do is to tell a Youtopian how much fun a product will be in a long, drawn-out, serious, or scholarly manner. He'll just look at you as if *you* dropped down from a strange planet.

4. Observe Youtopians in Their Secret Temples

In Youtopia, capitalism is the dominant religion. The high priest-practitioners of capitalism are those real estate developers, financial self-help gurus, and high-profile stock market analysts who have taken vows, first, to become richer than God, and then to help spread the gospel through their bestselling books. Youtopian citizens spend five days a week in their corporate temples, located at the World Materialism Center downtown. However, on the weekends, most Youtopians attend a secondary temple of some kind—either a gym, museum, or country club—where they can distance themselves from the sixty-hour-a-week rigors of worshipping at the Temple of Materialism (which occasionally makes them feel hollow inside—go figure).

These secondary temples have unofficial, codified languages that you will need to become fluent in if you are to succeed as a copywriter here in Youtopia. Feel free to eavesdrop, tap into the dominant concerns of the regular members, and then replay their hopes and fears back to them in all future communications. You will find several free passes in your Welcome Kit. (Please note that your observations will be far more accurate if you can manage to blend into your environment seamlessly. You may need to invest in certain liturgical garments to wear to these temples, such as ritzy gym clothes that cost more money than a copywriter earns in a week.)

5. Reach into the Cornucopia from Youtopia

With your Youtopian Transporter Device, Flattery Card, and free passes to many of the secret temples in the land, you now have all of the tools that you need to convert any Youtopian to your cause. These tools should work whether you are selling widgets or services that improve widgets exponentially. But if for some reason your first direct mail solicitation falls flat, don't be afraid to experiment with a different tactic. Did you promise a Youtopian that your product would be quick? Try switching your strategy in your follow-up communication and claim that it will be good for him instead. (Just don't say that it will be both quick and good for him.

Remember the two-word promise limit and stick to it!)

Now that you have learned basic copywriting, you should strive to attain the next level of mastery. Endeavor to think of yourself as an anthropologist. Use the techniques cited here to explore the minds of those to whom you are writing, and figure out which "hot buttons" to push. And what if your first letter succeeds beyond your wildest imaginings? First off, congratulations! (The Ministry of Information will be following up with a personalized Thank You note.) Second, don't be shy about reusing the winning tactic over and over again.

While life in Youtopia is constantly improving, at this minute, Youtopian society is still far from perfect. So, if your first letter happens to work gangbusters, please don't hesitate to stop all experiments and recycle, recycle, recycle. There's never a good reason to tamper with perfection!

The 7 Deadly Copywriting Sins

A clever adage refers to copywriting as "the unholy alliance of art and commerce." It's a colorful piece of language, implying that there are two sides waging war over every piece of business copy. On the Good Side stands the brave copywriter, valiantly defending his "creative" masterpiece against all of the dragons (otherwise known as clients and account people) in the advertising mash pit.

In reality, the opposite is true. When you work in an ad agency as a copywriter, you quickly learn that *everyone* is on the same side. In fact, there is a trinity of talented, driven people who will try to move Heaven and Earth so that your brilliant copy can ultimately propel sales into the stratosphere.

The clients tell you exactly what the product does. The planners tell you exactly what the ad is supposed to say. And the account people tell you everything else—who the market is (including age and zip code demographics), how consumers feel about your product (often in very emotional terms), and the strategy that you need to use (which is frequently a lot more creative than anything you could ever devise).

With the average length of an advertising headline just ten words long, and so many people around to help you write it, what could possibly go wrong?

Here are the seven deadly copywriting sins. (Please note that only some of them are committed exclusively by copywriters. There's enough guilt to go around for everyone involved.)

1. Pride

The client worked tirelessly for the last three years to improve his product (which he thinks of as his baby). As a result of his meticulous attention to detail, the product is six months late to market. By the time the new product is finally unveiled, the most brilliant ad in the universe can't motivate anyone to buy it because a similar product is already out there on the shelves. The window of opportunity has slammed shut.

Moral: Pride cometh before a fall. Get your product on the shelves in time or *sales will fall* drastically short of your goals.

2. Envy

Everyone involved in the marketing of a product, from the clients to the account people to the copywriter, secretly wishes that they could duplicate the smash success of Product X. So they roll up their shirtsleeves, sit down in a conference room together, and start brainstorming about X. After an hour, one of them suggests a selling platform that's nearly identical to X's. Everyone nods their heads sagely and goes home early that night. The problem is that the team is supposed to be selling Y, not X. In the ensuing print campaign, Y, trying to imitate X's marketing strategy, sounds like a copycat version of X, an X wanna-be. Instead of buying Y, consumers run out to buy more X.

Moral: Imitation is the sincerest way to sink a product's chances for survival.

3. Gluttony

During the past year, the ad agency's holding company swallowed another small ad agency. Or the ad agency was devoured by a large conglomerate. Or some investment bankers determined that the ad agency was too "bloated," and suggested that it start selling off its divisions. As a result, everyone working at the ad agency is far more worried about who might get axed in the merger or the specifics of the brand new profit sharing plan than about marketing, copywriting, or media placement. The resulting ad campaign is riddled with problems, from an unclear strategy to boring messaging to bizarre media selections. Consumers find the advertising uninspiring, or worse, just don't understand it.

Moral: Don't put too much on your plate. Advertising always needs to be priority number one.

4. Lust

The copywriter, secretly believing himself to be a creative superstar, needs to have his own suspicion validated. "Wouldn't it be great to walk away with a boatload of advertising awards for this campaign?" he asks himself. Instead of working hard to sell the product to the real people out there who can turn it into a success, he concentrates only on his own personal lust for accolades. He starts researching which fancy typefaces tend to win "creativity" awards rather than concentrating on selling the product. When the copywriter starts working for himself in this way, a lot of times the work he generates *does* end up winning creative awards. The judges of the advertising award show love the new advertising, but it's way too edgy or cerebral or "cool" for consumers. Sales drop, and the client ends up pulling the campaign.

Moral: Don't be tempted by the lure of creative awards. There is no relationship between awards and sales.

5. Anger

The good news is that the advertising campaign got noticed. Both the ad agency and the client company have received a slew of letters, most of them overwhelmingly positive. However, there are a couple of letters from consumers that are extremely negative. The large conservative client company, feeling prickly about receiving any negative feedback about the advertising, decides to pull the campaign prematurely. The "voice" of a very vocal minority has drowned out the pleased murmurs of the majority. Now there's an advertising blackout where no print campaigns run while the ad agency scrambles to come up with a new campaign.

Moral: You can't please all of the people all of the time. If an advertising campaign is working, stick with it.

6. Greed

In year one of a product's life cycle, sales vastly exceed the client's expectations. Suddenly, everyone's attention on the client side is focused on making the product an even bigger success in year two. Benchmarks are radically revised, goals are reset, there's a feeling of euphoria about the product that's impossible to contain. Because the new sales goals are completely unrealistic, the product vastly underperforms in year two. Now everyone on the client side feels like either the product is a loser or the ad agency is underperforming. The client calls an agency review and ultimately fires its advertising agency. While the proverbial baton shifts from one ad agency to the next, sales languish. It takes the new advertising agency six months to get up to speed on the product.

Moral: Don't let the desire for material gain cloud your rational judgment. Keep sales goals realistic.

7. Sloth

The advertising is working fairly well for a product. In the minds of the higher ups who run the account at the ad agency, that product is now on "cruise control." They shift their attention to a new business pitch or a glitzier, more exciting product, figuring that the first product is their bread and butter. By coincidence, one or two key players on the account leave the ad agency to pursue better jobs. Instead of replacing them with A players, the people running the business make some internal shifts, putting some B players in place to fill the void. When the new advertising is lackluster and sales plummet, everyone scratches their heads and wonders why.

Moral: Don't get lazy or have a cavalier attitude about success. Pay attention to your bread and butter accounts or there won't be any bread left to butter.

Contrary to popular belief, the alliance between art and commerce is *holy*. Everyone working on a particular product needs to attack its marketing with the passion of a zealot. Never take success for granted. Don't overreact to sales news (either good or bad). Stick to deadlines, and above all, concentrate on selling the product and you will be rewarded materially, and even spiritually (as long as the creative is relevant, engaging, and memorable).

Quick Word Finder:

An easy way to find exactly the word, or phrase, you're looking for.

hiseled crotchety ecstatic conscientious genuine dour gripping magnetic nagging erratic spiri
tenacity congenial titillating risque haughty enduring svelte poignant eccentric rich achieve as
nge chop clarify commit craft create dramatize enhance erase finagle find finesse generate ins
ogate interrupt jump lead motivate nip organize oversee pepper pinch plan raise rally rouse s
strategize surpass trump tweeze unveil win zoom striking appalling deadly manic inspired bleak r
disastrous exhilarating captivating outstanding wry chiseled crotchety ecstatic conscientious g
dour gripping magnetic nagging erratic spiritual cocky tenacity congenial titillating risque haug
ing svelte poignant eccentric rich achieve aspire challenge chop clarify commit craft create dra
nhance erase finagle find finesse generate inspire interrogate interrupt jump lead motivate nip org
ersee pepper pinch plan raise rally rouse save shake strategize surpass trump tweeze unveil
striking appalling deadly manic inspired bleak rigid jaded disastrous exhilarating captivating
ing wry chiseled crotchety ecstatic conscientious genuine dour gripping magnetic nagging err
ual cocky tenacity congenial titillating risque haughty enduring svelte poignant eccentric rich achi
e challenge chop clarify commit craft create dramatize enhance erase finagle find finesse gene
e interrogate interrupt jump lead motivate nip organize oversee pepper pinch plan raise rally ro
shake strategize surpass trump tweeze unveil win zoom striking appalling deadly manic inspired bl
jaded disastrous exhilarating captivating outstanding wry chiseled crotchety ecstatic conscient
ne dour gripping magnetic nagging erratic spiritual cocky tenacity congenial titillating risque hau
ing svelte poignant eccentric rich achieve aspire challenge chop clarify commit craft create dra
nhance erase finagle find finesse generate inspire interrogate interrupt jump lead motivate nip org
ersee pepper pinch plan raise rally rouse save shake strategize surpass trump tweeze unveil
striking appalling deadly manic inspired bleak rigid jaded disastrous exhilarating captivating
ing wry chiseled crotchety ecstatic conscientious genuine dour gripping magnetic nagging err
ual cocky tenacity congenial titillating risque haughty enduring svelte poignant eccentric rich ach
e challenge chop clarify commit craft create dramatize enhance erase finagle find finesse gene
e interrogate interrupt jump lead motivate nip organize oversee pepper pinch plan raise rally ro
shake nip striking appalling deadly manic inspired bleak rigid jaded disastrous exhilarating capti
utstanding wry chiseled crotchety ecstatic conscientious genuine dour gripping magnetic nag
ic spiritual cocky tenacity congenial titillating risque haughty enduring svelte poignant eccentric
ve aspire challenge chop clarify commit craft create dramatize enhance erase finagle find fine
rate inspire interrogate interrupt jump lead motivate nip organize oversee pepper pinch plan raise
e save shake strategize surpass trump tweeze unveil win zoom striking appalling deadly manic insp
rigid jaded disastrous exhilarating captivating outstanding wry chiseled crotchety ecstatic consc

chiseled crotchety ecstatic conscientious genuine dour gripping magnetic nagging erratic sp
ky tenacity congenial titillating risque haughty enduring svelte poignant eccentric rich achieve
llenge chop clarify commit craft create dramatize enhance erase finagle find finesse generate i
rrogate interrupt jump lead motivate nip organize oversee pepper pinch plan raise rally rouse
ke strategize surpass trump tweeze unveil win zoom striking appalling deadly manic inspired blea
d disastrous exhilarating captivating outstanding wry chiseled crotchety ecstatic conscientious
dour gripping magnetic nagging erratic spiritual cocky tenacity congenial titillating risque ha
uring svelte poignant eccentric rich achieve aspire challenge chop clarify commit craft create d
enhance erase finagle find finesse generate inspire interrogate interrupt jump lead motivate nip o
oversee pepper pinch plan raise rally rouse save shake strategize surpass trump tweeze unve
n striking appalling deadly manic inspired bleak rigid jaded disastrous exhilarating captivating
ding wry chiseled crotchety ecstatic conscientious genuine dour gripping magnetic nagging e
itual cocky tenacity congenial titillating risque haughty enduring svelte poignant eccentric rich ac
re challenge chop clarify commit craft create dramatize enhance erase finagle find finesse gen
ire interrogate interrupt jump lead motivate nip organize oversee pepper pinch plan raise rally
shake strategize surpass trump tweeze unveil win zoom striking appalling deadly manic inspired
jaded disastrous exhilarating captivating outstanding wry chiseled crotchety ecstatic conscier
uine dour gripping magnetic nagging erratic spiritual cocky tenacity congenial titillating risque ha
uring svelte poignant eccentric rich achieve aspire challenge chop clarify commit craft create dr
enhance erase finagle find finesse generate inspire interrogate interrupt jump lead motivate nip o
oversee pepper pinch plan raise rally rouse save shake strategize surpass trump tweeze unve
n striking appalling deadly manic inspired bleak rigid jaded disastrous exhilarating captivating
ding wry chiseled crotchety ecstatic conscientious genuine dour gripping magnetic nagging e
itual cocky tenacity congenial titillating risque haughty enduring svelte poignant eccentric rich ac
re challenge chop clarify commit craft create dramatize enhance erase finagle find finesse gen
ire interrogate interrupt jump lead motivate nip organize oversee pepper pinch plan raise rally r
shake nip striking appalling deadly manic inspired bleak rigid jaded disastrous exhilarating cap
outstanding wry chiseled crotchety ecstatic conscientious genuine dour gripping magnetic nag
tic spiritual cocky tenacity congenial titillating risque haughty enduring svelte poignant eccentric
eve aspire challenge chop clarify commit craft create dramatize enhance erase finagle find fir
erate inspire interrogate interrupt jump lead motivate nip organize oversee pepper pinch plan raise
e save shake strategize surpass trump tweeze unveil win zoom striking appalling deadly manic ins
k rigid jaded disastrous exhilarating captivating outstanding wry chiseled crotchety ecstatic cons
genuine dour gripping magnetic nagging erratic spiritual cocky tenacity congenial titillating

*About the Author

Vicky Oliver is an award-winning copywriter with X years of experience at brand-name, top-tier advertising agencies in Manhattan. She would confess how long she's been in the field, except that would go straight to her age—something she feels strongly that one should never have to reveal to anyone.

Ms. Oliver is an expert on all aspects of branding and has crafted TV, print, and radio campaigns for every product and service imaginable (except men's briefs). She has won numerous advertising awards—both for creativity and effectiveness. She has coined tag lines and named product lines for Fortune 500 companies. Her first book on the art of job hunting struck a real chord with readers throughout the country. After only a few short months on the shelves, *301 Smart Answers to Tough Interview Questions* went into its second printing.

Ms. Oliver has given seminars on "finding the brand that is you," job interviewing, and networking at The West Side Y in Manhattan. Her articles have been published in *Adweek* magazine and on *Crain's New York Business* website. She has appeared on national business TV programs (such as *Bloomberg TV*) and has been interviewed on both national and local radio stations over fifty times. Her advice was featured in the Sunday *New York Times*. Ms. Oliver's writings have put her in touch with over five thousand people in all different professions and in all walks of life: the employed, the unemployed, entrepreneurs, retirees, and freelancers.

A Brown University graduate with a degree in English Honors and a double major in political science, Ms. Oliver lives in New York City, where she has dedicated herself to helping others turn around their careers and their lives.

outstanding wry chiseled crotchety ecstatic conscientious genuine dour gripping
tic nagging erratic spiritual cocky tenacity congenial titillating risqué haughty end
elte poignant eccentric rich achieve aspire challenge chop clarify commit craft c
matize enhance erase finagle find finesse generate inspire interrogate interrupt
d motivate nip organize oversee pepper pinch plan raise rally rouse save shake st
e surpass trump tweeze unveil win zoom striking appalling deadly manic inspired
d jaded disastrous exhilarating captivating outstanding wry chiseled crotchety ecs
scientious genuine dour gripping magnetic nagging erratic spiritual cocky tenacity
nial titillating risqué haughty enduring svelte poignant eccentric rich achieve a
allenge chop clarify commit craft create dramatize enhance erase finagle find fir
nerate inspire interrogate interrupt jump lead motivate nip organize oversee pe
ch plan raise rally rouse save shake strategize surpass trump tweeze unveil win
king appalling deadly manic inspired bleak rigid jaded disastrous exhilarating cap
outstanding wry chiseled crotchety ecstatic conscientious genuine dour gripping
tic nagging erratic spiritual cocky tenacity congenial titillating risqué haughty end
elte poignant eccentric rich achieve aspire challenge chop clarify commit craft c
matize enhance erase finagle find finesse generate inspire interrogate interrupt
d motivate nip organize oversee pepper pinch plan raise rally rouse save shake st
e surpass trump tweeze unveil win zoom striking appalling deadly manic inspired
d jaded disastrous exhilarating captivating outstanding wry chiseled crotchety ecs
scientious genuine dour gripping magnetic nagging erratic spiritual cocky tenacity
nial titillating risqué haughty enduring svelte poignant eccentric rich achieve a
allenge chop clarify commit craft create dramatize enhance erase finagle find fir
nerate inspire interrogate interrupt jump lead motivate nip organize oversee pe
ch plan raise rally rouse save shake strategize surpass trump tweeze unveil win
king appalling deadly manic inspired bleak rigid jaded disastrous exhilarating cap
outstanding wry chiseled crotchety ecstatic conscientious genuine dour gripping
tic nagging erratic spiritual cocky tenacity congenial titillating risqué haughty end
elte poignant eccentric rich achieve aspire challenge chop clarify commit craft c
matize enhance erase finagle find finesse generate inspire interrogate interrupt
motivate nip organize oversee pepper pinch plan raise rally rouse save shake nip